The
DEVASTATED
VINEYARD

BOOKS BY DIETRICH VON HILDEBRAND

Aesthetik (2 vols.)
The Art of Living*
Celibacy and the Crisis of Faith*
In Defense of Purity*
Ethics*
The Encyclical "Humanae Vitae": a Sign of Contradiction*
Engelbert Dollfuss: Christlicher Staatsmann
Fundamental Moral Attitudes
Graven Images: Substitutes for True Morality
Die Idee der sittlichen Handlung
Das Katholische Berufsethos
Liturgy and Personality
Man and Woman*
Marriage
Die Menschheit am Scheideweg
Metaphysik der Gemeinschaft
Morality and Situation Ethics*
Mozart, Beethoven, Schubert
The New Tower of Babel
Not as the World Gives*
The Sacred Heart
Sittlichkeit und ethische Werterkenntnis
Der Sinn philosophischen Fragens und Erkennens
Transformation in Christ*
The Trojan Horse in the City of God*
What is Philosophy?*
Das Wesen der Liebe

In preparation:
Epistemological Investigations
Memoirs
Metaphysics
Moralia
Philosophy of Logic and Language

---

*Published by Franciscan Herald Press, Chicago, Ill.

The

DEVASTATED

VINEYARD

Dietrich von Hildebrand

Translated from the German
by John Crosby, Ph.D., and Fred Teichert, Ph.D.

FRANCISCAN HERALD PRESS
1434 WEST 51st STREET ● CHICAGO, 60609

The Devastated Vineyard, by Dietrich von Hildebrand. English version of *Der verwuestete Weinberg* (Regensburg: Josef Habbel, 1973). Translated from the German by John Crosby, Ph.D. and Fred Teichert, Ph.D. Copyright © 1973 by Franciscan Herald Press, 1434 West 51st Street, Chicago, Illinois 60609.

Library of Congress Cataloging in Publication Data:

Von Hildebrand, Dietrich, 1889-
    The devastated vineyard.

        Translation of Der verwüstete Weinberg.
        1. Catholic Church — Doctrinal and controversial works — Catholic authors. I. Title.
BX1751.2.V6613   201.'1   73-18117
ISBN 0-8199-0462-7

Dilectissimae amicae

in Jesu Christo D. N.

Mädl

Contents

‼‼

Preface ix

Introduction xi

PART I

Chapter

1. The Lethargy of the Guardians 3
2. Is There One Contemporary Philosophy? 8
3. The False Idea of a Middle Way
   between Extremes 15
4. The Great Illusion 20
5. Is There Still a Ray of Light? 52
6. Is History the Source of Revelation? 55
7. "Qui te fecit sine te . . ." 61
8. The Great Disappointment 66
9. Change for Its Own Sake 78
10. The Idolization of Learning 83
11. "Ecumenitis" 91
12. Is Schism the Greatest Evil? 98
13. Dawn 102

PART II

Chapter

14. The Sacred Humanity of Jesus 109
15. This-Worldliness 127
16. Distortion of Morality and of Love of Neighbor 141
17. Is Unity among the Faithful the Highest Value? 158
18. The Cult of the "Positive" 165
19. The Eruption of Collectivism in the
    Holy Church 182
20. Democratization of the Holy Church 195
21. Fear of Using the Authority of the Holy Church 202
22. False Interpretation of Authority 210
23. The Catchword "Ghetto" 214
24. Cooperation with Atheists? 217
25. Harmless Religion 223
26. The Message of the "Our Father" 232
27. How God Wants Us to Respond in the
    Present Crisis 244

Preface

TODAY WE CAN no longer call the situation in the holy Church "The Trojan Horse in the City of God." The enemies who were hidden in the Trojan Horse have stepped out of their encasement and the active work of destruction is in high gear. The epidemic has advanced from scarcely recognizable errors and falsifications of the spirit of Christ and the holy Church, up to the most flagrant heresies and blasphemies.

On the other hand, however, a great and promising improvement can be noted. The danger which threatens the holy Church from within is being recognized more and more. Many who were originally deceived by such slogans as "renewal," "*aggiornamento*," and "come out of the ghetto," have returned to orthodoxy. Various movements have been formed which are taking the offensive against the destruction of the holy Church and the falsification of the Christian spirit; and above all, men in high ecclesiastical offices are also raising their voices now. The situation today has become even more clearly one of open battle between Satan and

Christ, between the Spirit of the World and the Spirit of the holy Church.

The purpose of this book is, first of all, to give a short, clear presentation of the principal errors which are being presented today as a breakthrough to the "modern" man who has "come of age," whom one can supposedly no longer expect to believe the teaching of the Church in the form it has taken up to now. These are errors which in reality, however, are in no way new, and some of them have been expressly condemned by the Council of Trent, some by the First Vatican Council. We may thus speak here of forgotten anathemas. Secondly, we shall especially try to unmask those hidden, subtle errors which are usually introduced under beautiful, apparently noble titles, and whose danger is often overlooked even by believing Catholics.

The awakening of many to all this, however, and the opposition which is growing daily to the distortion of the true spirit of the Gospels and of the holy Church must at the present time fill us with hope. This, too, will be discussed briefly in this book.

Against the background of the glory of Divine Revelation, of the miracle and the inconceivable gift which is the holy Church, of the saints' victorious conquest over the spirit of the world, I want to show clearly what a disaster it is that such grave errors and such mediocrity have penetrated into the Church, and then I want to show that the steadily growing opposition to the devastation of the vineyard of the Lord is a kind of dawn, a consoling source of genuine hope for us. If I should succeed in this, then this book will have achieved its aim.

Introduction

AN UNPREJUDICED look at the present devastation of the vineyard of the Lord cannot fail to notice the fact that a "fifth column" has formed within the Church, a group which consciously aims at systematically destroying her. (They are referred to as the "Mafia" by some, including authorities in the Church.) We have already pointed this out in earlier works. One alarming symptom is the fact that priests, theologians, and bishops who have lost their faith do not leave the Church, but rather remain within her — and indeed play the role of saviors of the Church in the modern world. Why do they not openly leave the Church, like Voltaire, Renan, and many others?

Their systematic and artful undermining of the holy Church testifies clearly enough to the fact that this is a conscious conspiracy, involving Freemasons and Communists who, in spite of their differences and usual enmity in other matters, are working together toward this goal. For the Church is the arch-enemy of Freemasonry,[1] and is the principal hindrance to the Communists in their conquest of the world. Naturally the

Communists are incomparably more dangerous, but Free-masonry, though in theory not so clearly antithetical to Christianity, is a welcome co-worker in the "fifth column."

The inconceivable thing is that this conspiracy exists within the Church, that there are bishops and even cardinals, and many priests and religious, who play the role of Judas.[2] That such a "fifth column" exists is not merely my unauthoritative private opinion; on the contrary, a number of cardinals, bishops, and prelates have declared in private conversations that no one who is not blind can overlook this incredibly tightly organized "fifth column" within the Church. Of course the number of religious who belong to this "fifth column" may be comparatively small, but they have a clear aim, coupled with the kind of intelligence that one finds in all Soviet and Chinese embassies, which should be more precisely characterized as slyness and cunning, to distinguish it from true intelligence.

It must be emphasized from the outset, however, that the destruction of the Church is being sought from two completely different motives. In one case it is the conspiracy which has existed at all times to undermine the Faith and destroy the Church, with the sole difference that those involved do not want to undermine the Church from without, but rather from within. This is precisely the system of the "fifth column." People who pretend to be Catholics, who assume offices in the Church, are seeking from within, under the banner of reform and progress, to destroy the Church.

Completely different from these people are those who do not want to destroy the Church as such, i.e., who do not seek the disappearance of the Church, but who rather want to transform the Church into something which completely contradicts her meaning and essence. This includes all those who wish to make the Church of Jesus Christ into a purely humanitarian society, to rob her of her supernatural character, to secularize and desacralize her. They share that camouflage of the enemies of the Church which comes from using the shibboleths of "reform," "progress," and "adaptation to modern man." But they do not want to eliminate the Church. The catchwords "reform" and "progress" are not mere tricks which they use; they really believe them.

The result of the activity of this group is the same as that of the first group; only their motives are different. This latter group would vehemently protest if one were to accuse them of intending the destruction of the Church. But they have lost the true Christian Faith to such an extent that they do not clearly understand that the secularized, humanitarian organization which they want to make out of the holy Church would have nothing left in common with the Church of Jesus Christ. They do not see that if they were to reach their goal, it would amount to the destruction of the Church.

Henri de Lubac, S.J., pointed this out with forceful and penetrating words:

"One becomes conscious that the Church is confronted with a grave crisis. In the name of a "new" Church, a "postconciliar" Church, some people are attempting to found another Church than that of Jesus Christ: an anthropocentric society, which is threatened by an 'immanentist apostasy,' and which can be drawn into a movement of general surrender under the cloak of rejuvenation, ecumenism, or adaptation."[3]

NOTES

1. The enmity of freemasonry to the Church has been well documented by Bishop Graber of Regensburg in his outstanding book, *Athanasius und die Kirche seiner Zeit* (Abensberg: Josef Kral Verlag, 1973), especially in the chapter, "Geheime Gesellschaften."

2. But this is by no means the first time that the Church has had enemies within. St. Basil wrote in 373 of the Arian heresy: "For when the devil saw that the Church was growing and flourishing in the persecutions of the pagans, he changed his tactics and decided not to fight the Church so openly; he now secretly devises snares for us and hides his treachery behind the high-sounding names which he has given them. And so, while we suffer the same things which our fathers once suffered, we do not seem to suffer for Christ's sake, for our persecutors call themselves Christians." Quoted by Bishop Graber, *ibid.,* p. 24.

3. Père Henri de Lubac, S.J., from a speech given at the World Congress of Theology in Toronto (August, 1967), quoted in the *Témoignage Chrétien* (Paris), Sept. 1, 1967.

PART I

1

The Lethargy of the Guardians

:::

ONE OF THE MOST horrifying and widespread diseases in the Church today is the lethargy of the guardians of the Faith of the Church. I am not thinking here of those bishops who are members of the "fifth column," who wish to destroy the Church from within, or to transform it into something completely different. I am thinking of the far more numerous bishops who have no such intentions, but who make no use whatever of their authority when it comes to intervening against heretical theologians or priests, or against blasphemous performances of public worship. They either close their eyes and try, ostrich-style, to ignore the grievous abuses as well as appeals to their duty to intervene, or they fear to be attacked by the press or the mass media and defamed as reactionary, narrow-minded, or medieval. They fear men more than God. The words of St. John Bosco apply to them: "The power of evil men lives on the cowardice of the good."

It is certainly true that the lethargy of those in positions of authority is a disease of our times which is widespread outside the Church. It is found among parents, college and university presidents, heads of numerous other organizations, judges, heads of state, and others. But the fact that this sickness has even penetrated the Church is a clear indication that the fight against the spirit of the world, has been replaced with swimming along with the spirit of the times in the name of *"aggiornamento."* One is forced to think of the hireling who abandons his flocks to the wolves when one reflects on the lethargy of so many bishops and superiors who, though still orthodox[1] themselves, do not have the courage to intervene against the most flagrant heresies and abuses of all kinds in their dioceses or in their orders.

But it is most especially infuriating when certain bishops, who themselves show this lethargy toward heretics, assume a rigorously authoritarian attitude toward those believers who are fighting for orthodoxy, and who are thus doing what the bishops ought to be doing themselves! I was once allowed to read a letter written by a man in high position in the Church, addressed to a group which had heroically taken up the cause of the true Faith, of the pure, true teaching of the Church and the Pope. This group had overcome the "cowardice of good men" of which St. John Bosco spoke, and ought thus to have been the greatest joy of the bishops. The letter said: as good Catholics, you have to do only one thing: just be obedient to all the ordinances of your bishop.

This conception of a "good" Catholic is particularly surprising at a time in which the coming of age of the modern layman is continually being emphasized. But it is also completely false for this reason: what is fitting at a time when no heresies occur in the Church without being immediately condemned by Rome, becomes inappropriate and unconscionable at a time when uncondemned heresies wreak havoc within the Church, infecting even certain bishops, who nevertheless remain in office. Should the faithful at the time of the Arian heresy, for instance, in which the majority of the bishops were Arians, have limited themselves to being nice, and obedient to the ordinances of these bishops, instead of battling the heresy? Is not fidelity to the true teaching of the Church to be given priority over submission to the bishop? Is it not precisely by virtue of their obedience to the revealed truths which they received from the magisterium of the Church, that the faithful offer resistance? Are the faithful not supposed to be concerned when things are preached from the pulpit which are completely incompatible with the teaching of the Church? Or when theologians are kept on as teachers who claim that the Church must accept pluralism in philosophy and theology,⁵ or that there is no survival of the person after death, or who deny that promiscuity is a sin, or even tolerate public displays of immorality, thereby betraying a pitiful lack of understanding for the deeply Christian virtue of purity?

The drivel of the heretics, both priests and laymen, is tolerated; the bishops tacitly acquiesce to the poisoning of the faithful.⁶ But they want to silence the faithful believers who take up the cause of orthodoxy, the very people who should by all rights be the joy of the bishops' hearts, their consolation, a source of strength for overcoming their own lethargy. Instead, these people are regarded as disturbers of the peace. And should it happen that they get carried away in their zeal and express themselves in a tactless or exaggerated manner, they are even suspended. This clearly shows the cowardice which is hidden behind the bishops' failure to use their authority. For they have nothing to fear from the orthodox; the orthodox do not control the mass media or the press; they are not the representatives of public opinion. And because of their submission to ecclesiastical authority, the fighters for orthodoxy will never be as aggressive as the so-called progressives. If they are reprimanded or disciplined, their bishops run no risk of being attacked by the liberal press and being defamed as reactionary.

This failure of the bishops to make use of their God-given authority is perhaps, in practical consequences, the worst confusion in the Church today. For this failure not only does not arrest spiritual diseases, heresies, and the blatant as well as the insidious (and this is much worse) devastation of the vineyard of the Lord; it even gives free rein to these evils. The failure to use holy authority to protect the holy Faith leads necessarily to the disintegration of the Church.

Here, as with the appearance of all dangers, we have to say, *"principiis obsta"* ("stop the evil at its source"). The longer one allows an evil to develop, the more difficult it will be to root it out again. This is true for the upbringing of children, for the life of the state, and in a special way for the moral life of the individual. But it is true in a completely new way for the intervention of the ecclesiastical authorities for the good of the faithful. As Plato says, "when evils are far advanced, . . . it is never pleasant to eliminate them."[7]

Nothing is more erroneous than to imagine that many things ought to be allowed to rage and do their worst, and that one ought thus to wait patiently until they subside of their own accord. This theory may sometimes be correct with regard to youths going through puberty, but it is completely false in questions of the *bonum commune* (the common good). This false theory is especially dangerous when applied to the *bonum commune* of the holy Church, involving blasphemies in public worship and heresies which, if not condemned, go on poisoning countless souls. Here it is incorrect to apply the parable of the wheat and the tares.

NOTES

4. By "orthodox" we mean the belief in the unfalsified, official teaching of the holy Church, which represents the authentic, revealed Truth, guaranteed by the Holy Spirit. The expression "orthodox" in no way refers here to membership in the schismatic Eastern Church.

5. By "pluralism" I mean the notion that one can have different opinions and views with regard to defined truths of faith, or that every philosophy has a place in the Church — ultimately an absolute relativism. Of course as long as no definition has been given concerning a pure question of faith, different opinions may also be advocated by orthodox Catholics. Thus, with regard to the Immaculate Conception of the Blessed Virgin Mary, contradictory opinions were held by St. Thomas and Duns Scotus. But after the definition of 1854 this would no longer have been possible. Similarly, as we will see, there are philosophical theses only one of which can be true, but neither of which is in contradiction to the Revelation of Christ. But this kind of pluralism is clearly different from the pluralism advocated by Rahner and others.

6. A shocking example of the activity of the "fifth column" in the Church are the religion books recently introduced in Austria: *Glaube Gefragt* ("Faith Questioned") and *Christus Gefragt* ("Christ Questioned"). These books are consciously aimed at the destruction of the Faith in the souls of the young. This is also a crass example of the lethargy of the guardians.

7. Plato, *Laws*, no. 660.

2

Is There One Contemporary Philosophy?

::

IN OUR BOOK ENTITLED *Trojan Horse in the City of God,*
and in the introduction to *Celibacy and the Crisis of Faith,*
we spoke of many of the bad tendencies and grave heretical
errors which were and still are wreaking havoc in the post-
conciliar Church. Nowadays they are no longer being proclaimed so much as great novelties and discoveries, but rather
are assumed by many to be self-evident and to require no
further discussion. This is also true of the theories of the
arch-heresiarch, Teilhard de Chardin.

In his book, *Mein Kampf,* Hitler wrote that if one repeats
something continually, even if it is not in fact true, it will
nevertheless ultimately be considered self-evident. This ob-
servation about the way in which the masses can be influenced is perhaps the only true thing to be found in this
deplorable book.

We fully intend to analyze dangerous new tendencies and
disastrous errors; however, let us again note two fundamental

points briefly at the outset: the legend or myth of "modern" man, and historical relativism.

We showed in *Trojan Horse* and *Celibacy and the Crisis of Faith* that this "modern man" does not exist. He is an inveniton of the sociologists.

"As long as one only refers to the immense change in the external conditions of life brought about by the enormous technological development which has taken place, then one is referring to an indubitable fact. But this outward change has had no fundamental influence on man — on his essential nature, on the sources of his happiness, on the meaning of his life, on the metaphysical situation of man. And yet only some such fundamental change in man would have any bearing at all on his ability to understand the language in which the Church has been announcing the Gospel of Christ to mankind for thousands of years.

"A modern knowledge of history and an unprejudiced view of it could not fail to convince anyone that the 'modern man' who is radically different from the men of all other periods is a pure invention, or rather, a typical myth."[8]

As to historical relativism, which unfortunately is influencing many Catholic theologians, let us emphasize once again how serious this is, and how radically incompatible with the Revelation of Christ. Here objective truth is replaced by historical-sociological "reality":

"This historical aliveness of certain ideologies and attitudes [is confused with] their truth, validity, and value. The categories of truth and falsity have been replaced by the question of whether something is effective in the present age or belongs to a former age, whether it is current or superannuated, 'alive' or 'dead.' Whether something is alive and 'dynamic' seems more important than whether it is true and good. This substitution is an obvious symptom of intellectual and moral decay. In former times, when certain ideas and ideals gained a great influence over many minds because of their historical vigor, their adherents were nevertheless convinced of their truth and value. But today, the interpersonal, historical reality of an idea is alone enough to cause people to rave about it and feel sheltered in it. . . . The most striking example of the exclusive interest in historical-social aliveness [and the concomitant elimination of the question of truth] is the 'God is dead' drivel, and the extent to which this expression is taken seriously."[9]

But we must discuss in greater detail an aspect of this dependence on the spirit of the age which we have not yet discussed as such. One can often hear the opinion, even from Catholics who still hold fast to the *depositum catholicae fidei* (deposit of Catholic faith), that it is praiseworthy of many theologians to build bridges to contemporary philosophy, to express the message of Christ, without of course sacrificing any of its content, in the language and with the concepts of contemporary philosophy.

And here the question arises: is there any such thing as a single contemporary philosophy?

No, there is truly not one contemporary philosophy. We find in many epochs of history different and sometimes fundamentally opposed philosophies. One may be more widespread and have more adherents, but a variety of schools of thought has characterized every era in which there was active philosophical inquiry. Parmenides and Heraclitus, who were certainly different and indeed opposed in their philosophies, belong more or less to the same historical epoch. The same is true of Socrates and the Sophists. How many different and opposing schools of philosophical thought we find in Hellenism! But at the present time less than ever before can one speak of a contemporary philosophy — insofar as one can still speak of philosophy at all in the authentic sense of the word. Our epoch contains completely different and opposing philosophies. We find positivistic empiricists of all varieties, pragmatists, logical positivists, all kinds of materialists, disciples of Kant, Hegel, and Heidegger, Thomists such as Maritain, Gilson, and Marcel de Corte, thinkers like Gabriel Marcel who cannot be classified in any school, and finally, those who are exponents of Augustinian realism. Which one is *the* contemporary philosophy?

At most one could speak of certain characteristics which are found in many of the above listed philosophies, such as immanentism and subjectivism, epistemological and historical relativism, moral relativism and atheism. These disastrous errors can indeed be found in many of the above-named philosophical schools. But, thank God, there are many other schools in which they cannot be found, such as among the Thomists, or Gabriel Marcel, and especially those defenders of objective truth who have a deep affinity with St. Augustine.

Divine Revelation presupposes implicitly certain absolute fundamental truths which can be known by natural reason. As I pointed out in chapter six of the *Trojan Horse,* all forms of relativism, immanentism, materialism, determinism, and subjectivism are absolutely incompatible with Christian Revelation. It is nonsense to assume that, instead of refuting these errors on a purely rational level, instead of unmasking their completely unproved character and even their inner contradictions, one can "build bridges" to them, and that one ought to formulate the teaching of the Church in a terminology which has been molded by these errors. And it is a pure illusion to expect thereby to be better understood by our contemporaries and especially to pave the way for them to the true Faith.

The devastation of the vineyard of the Lord is manifested in a most disastrous way in progressivist theology. In *The Trojan Horse in the City of God* we have already pointed out many of these heresies. The apostasy from the true Faith, which is not conceded to be apostasy by those who proclaim it but is interpreted instead as *aggiornamento,* has become much more widespread since 1967. It has increased alarmingly both in extent, as well as in distance from authentic Christian belief. If we think of the pluralism of Rahner, or of Schillebeeckx's denial of the immortality of the soul and of the difference between body and soul, or Marlet's denial of a transcendent God, or the claim of Gregory Baum that God reveals Himself in the spirit of the age, or Küng's denial of the infallibility of the Church in matters of faith and morals, or many others, then we can see with shocking clarity how the devastation of the vineyard of the Lord is progressing. It is shocking because all these theologians are continuing to hold classes and to give lectures and to proclaim themselves Catholics — shocking because they have neither been relieved of their offices and suspended, nor officially condemned. How can this irresponsible activity in the area of theology do anything else but slowly ruin and destroy the Church?

It certainly happened in certain epochs in which there was a great fear of heresy, that many things were wrongly believed to be incompatible with the teaching of the Church. Thus it is just not possible to interpret Descartes' writings as incompatible with the teaching of the Church, if they are correctly understood and judged in themselves and not according to their historical influence. This is not by any means to say that errors do not crop up in his philosophy alongside his great insights. But the question here is whether a thesis contains a contradiction to the fundamental natural truths which are tacitly presupposed in the Revelation of Christ.

But as soon as it is a question of a philosophical school which, as mentioned above, is absolutely incompatible with Christian Revelation, then there can be no pluralism in the Church. A philosophy such as Spinoza's, in which God is not a person and man has no free will and indeed is not a substance at all, can never be objectively reconciled with the *depositum catholicae fidei.*

As regrettable as was the overly anxious attitude of the Church in certain epochs, and the widespread mistrust of all philosophy which was not strictly Thomistic, nevertheless this narrowness still cannot be compared with the evil of present-day "pluralism." It leads to terrible consequences when philosophies which are absolutely incompatible with the deposit of the Catholic Faith, such as all varieties of transcendental idealism and even out and out relativism, can be taught at Catholic universities without hindrance. Though these theories may be branded as false by the Holy Father when speaking to a small group, nevertheless as long as those espousing such philosophies, be they laymen or priests, are permitted to teach at institutions which call themselves Catholic, they can effortlessly undermine the faith of countless people and also destroy all sense of how irreconcilable certain false philosophies are with the orthodox Faith. A kind of·schizophrenia is being bred through all this.

An unfortunate false notion of *caritas,* an over-emphasis on unity at the expense of truth, a false irenicism: all these are reasons for the tendency to want to unite irreconcilable things for as long as possible. Whereas the former narrowness was no danger to orthodoxy, the toleration of the spreading of theories which are in contradiction to the deposit of the Catholic Faith presents a mortal danger to orthodoxy.

NOTES

8. Dietrich von Hildebrand, *Celibacy and the Crisis of Faith* (Chicago: Franciscan Herald Press, 1971), pp. XIV-XV.

9. Dietrich von Hildebrand, *The Trojan Horse in the City of God* (Chicago: Franciscan Herald Press, 1967), pp. 82-83.

3
The False Idea of a Middle Way between Extremes

ONE CAN SOMETIMES hear propounded the unfortunate thesis that opposite errors are equally dangerous. It is assumed that because something is false or exaggerated, because one renounces it as "extremist," that its opposite must be just as false and dangerous. It is forgotten that there is a hierarchy of evils, a hierarchy of dangers; and the fact that these evils and errors are opposite, in no way proves that they are equally evil, and equally dangerous.

A heresy cannot be placed on the same level as an undesirable attitude of mind. If I juxtapose laxity and rigorism, I can call the former "too little" and the latter "too much" — but never can a heresy be compared in this way to a narrow-minded attitude which represents no heresy.

In relation to heresies there is no *minus malum,* no "lesser evil" — apart from the fact that certain heresies can be weightier and worse than others.

15

In politics the insight that there is a *minus malum* is indispensable and basic. But if it is a matter of opposed tendencies in the Church, then the decisive difference is whether they are heretical, or only unfortunate, exaggerated, narrow-minded. A short while ago, a well-known and important French theologian, who deplores the present devastation of the vineyard of the Lord, said to me that the "integrists" were just as bad as the modernists. According to him, the integrists, who see everything which is not strictly Thomistic as heretical, were, through their spiritual and intellectual narrowness, as great a danger as the "progressivists," who want to introduce a pluralism into the holy Church — or a Hans Küng, who denies the infallibility of the Church.

This is obviously a great error. The narrowness of the integrists may be regrettable, but it is not heretical. It is not incompatible with the teaching of the holy Church. It views certain philosophical theses as inseparable from orthodoxy, though they in no way are. But these philosophical theses are also in no way incompatible with Christian Revelation. Therefore, it is completely senseless to place those who hold a philosophic thesis to be inseparable from Christian Revelation, i.e., from the teaching of the holy Church, on a level with those who promulgate philosophic theses which are in radical contradiction to the teaching of the holy Church, of which we spoke in the last chapter.

But there are many philosophical questions which do not have this relation to Christian Revelation. To be sure, the alternatives of the truth or falsity of the thesis remain, but its compatibility with orthodoxy is not at stake. Whether someone accepts the thesis that *nil erit in intellectu quod non fuerit in sensibus,*[10] or whether he concurs with the Augustinian view on this point, has nothing to do with orthodoxy.

But it is not difficult to see that whoever believes and proclaims fundamental errors which are absolutely incompatible with Christian Revelation is clearly a heretic, whereas someone who holds philosophical theses to be indispensable which in themselves have no necessary relation to Christian Revelation, becomes thereby in no way a heretic.

But apart from the grave mistake of placing both on the same level with regard to content, it is still a great mistake to believe that the integrists, who have always been present, and who are pious, orthodox men, are just as dangerous to the Church as the declared heretics, including many who want to demolish the Church (the "fifth column") or to remake her according to their own theories. This attack from within is being conducted with all available means and propagated by the mass media; it is an epidemic which is growing more widespread every day. This is a real danger, a disintegration of the Church. With the integrists, on the other hand, there can be no question of such a danger.

But there can be very different reasons for this shortsightedness of equating two so incomparable evils. I am speaking here only of cases in which, for example, a completely orthodox priest, who deeply deplores all the present-day heresies, falls victim to the theory that both extremes are equally dangerous and that truth lies in the middle.

One reason is that often the *mesotes theory*,[11] which indeed is applicable to many spheres, is carelessly extended to spheres where it does not apply at all. We have discussed this in detail in *The Trojan Horse*, where we said that truth does not lie in the middle between two extremes, but is rather above and beyond them. While I can meaningfully say that something should not be too cold and not too warm, not too bright and not too dark, not too salty and not too bland, it makes no sense to say that one should not be too pious or not pious enough, too virtuous or not virtuous enough. All the more is it meaningless to say that this person is too orthodox and that one is not orthodox enough and to claim that truth lies in the middle. Orthodoxy *is* the truth and all heresies are not forms of extremism, they are not exaggerations; they are simply false, incompatible with the Revelation of Christ. It may be that psychologically one heresy springs from an over-emphasis of one truth at the expense of another. But the heresy itself cannot ever be viewed as one extreme to which is opposed the contrary extreme of "too orthodox." Rather, it is just false, not true.

There is another reason why many have been seduced into placing incomparable errors on the same level, and it is purely psychological in nature. Men who have had to suffer much under the narrowness of spirit of the extremists, and who have been unjustly suspected of being heretics, have developed such an antipathy toward this fanaticism, and they shun and fear it so much, that they are inclined to put this evil on the same level as grave errors of faith, or indeed, as explicit heresies. It is actually quite seldom the case that men are completely objective in their judgments. Personal experiences, especially the most painful ones, usually play a role, and make an evil seem to be greater than it objectively is, or *vice-versa*. If one is treated in a friendly and respectful manner by a person, one will pass more favorable judgment on this person or the school of thought which he represents, although one had once seen the danger of it clearly, and although it has not in reality changed in any respect.

To take another example, the judgment of superiors or bishops is often clouded because they believe that obedience and submission are more important than orthodoxy. Of course, I am thinking here only of those who are orthodox themselves and who deplore all heresies. But the insult to God which is embodied in heresy is often not as tangible and irritating for them as a public act of rebellion against their authority. Certainly they should also make use of their authority if their subordinates are disobedient. But first priority in authoritative intervention must be given to the question of whether the subordinate champions the truth in matters of faith and morals.

A person who, because he has suffered from the narrowness of the "integrists," regards them as just as dangerous as the progressives, is guilty of a lack of objectivity similar to that of such bishops.

By the way, there is much talk of the legalism which must be overcome. Indeed, many even describe the Decalogue as legalistic. But in truth a greater, more real legalism has come into being since the Second Vatican Council. We have just pointed to one symptom of real legalism in the negative sense: that more use of authority is being made in purely disciplinary matters than in matters of faith. The belief that a lack of discipline is more serious than the spread of heresies is a typical form of legalism. All disciplinary authority, all obedience to the bishop presupposes the pure teaching of the holy Church. Obedience to the bishop is grounded in complete faith in the teachings of the holy Church. As soon as the ecclesiastical authority yields to a pluralism in questions of faith, it has lost the right to claim obedience to its disciplinary ordinances.

NOTES

10. "Nothing can be in the intellect which was not first in the senses."
11. The Aristotelian idea that virtue lies in the mean between two extremes.

4
The Great Illusion

:::

HAND IN HAND with the unfortunate "myth of modern man," to which I have drawn attention in *The Trojan Horse in the City of God* and in *Celibacy and the Crisis of Faith,* goes the disastrous idea of the great progress man is supposed to have achieved in the present day. The illusion that our time represents progress in comparison with earlier times is an important factor in the devastation of the vineyard of the Lord. In *The Trojan Horse,* Chapter 17, we discussed the essence of true progress in detail. We spoke of progress in an absolute sense, such as progress in the sanctification of the soul of the individual person and in the spreading of the Kingdom of God on earth, i.e., the growth of the Mystical Body of Christ, the holy Church, and we distinguished this from progress for all human life and happiness. Finally, we spoke of immanent progress in a special area, such as natural science, technology, and medicine.

We have also discussed the erroneous character of the

Hegelian theory of the development of the World Spirit, as well as that of the much farther-reaching evolutionary progress in Teilhard de Chardin.

Here we do not intend to go into these false theories again in detail; they have no objective foundations whatever. Rather, let us examine the blindness regarding the present state of the world, the conceit, "how marvelously far we have come," to quote Famulus Wagner in *Faust*, the concretely false evaluation of our epoch and all its tendencies. We intend to try to elaborate briefly on the true situation of humanity today in comparison with former times, and to show how impossible it is to speak of progress on the whole.

Let us first of all consider forms of immanent progress within a particular realm. Thus we note without a doubt the enormous progress in the spheres of medicine and technology, and in many of the natural sciences. This kind of progress, which has an almost automatic character about it, and besides occurs in shorter and shorter periods of time, gives the present epoch a glorious appearance.

On the other hand, what price is being paid for this progress? This is quite another matter. Many of these advances, while they present numerous advantages and conveniences for human life, nevertheless entail great disadvantages as well.[12] Ecology speaks of these disadvantages; they are so great that they threaten to destroy the physical existence of mankind. To mention just one example: the pollution of the atmosphere by factories and automobiles, the killing of fish and other living creatures in lakes, in rivers, and on the seashore by all the chemical products in the sewage.

But from a human point of view, many of the achievements of modern technology bring both advantages and disadvantages at the same time. For example, the electric light undoubtedly makes life easier in comparison with illumination by petroleum lamps or candles. But on the other hand it considerably reduces the freedom of the individual. Countless people can be left in darkness if something goes wrong at the central power plant. As long as each person had his own petroleum lamp or candle, he was not dependent on a central power plant. The same is true of the water supply. Max Scheler has already drawn attention to the fact that the advances in technology make the life of the individual more comfortable, but they are simultaneously paid for by a reduction of freedom.

Then, too, valuable technical discoveries are coupled with disadvantages on the human level from a completely different point of view. The automobile is certainly a great gift for man, even apart from the advantages of comfort and practicality. By means of the automobile we are able to come to an intimate knowledge of countries with very beautiful landscapes. This, in comparison to what was afforded by the train, is a great gift for many, especially for those who have a deep sense of beauty in nature and architecture, for it makes possible a much more intimate contact with these things. But technical progress has killed much of the intimacy of this very contact; the traveler's separation from the living environment turns out to be just as great as it was with the train. In addition, the resulting temptation to drive with great speed on a freeway further reduces the intimacy of the contact with surrounding nature. It is the old conflict between utility and deep contact with values. If I must reach a certain goal, speed is a great advantage. But for the full life, for the experience of deep impressions, for being caught up by the reality which surrounds us, for the priceless gift of experiencing the present moment, a trip in the time of Goethe was of course incomparably more delightful and fruitful. There is an enormous difference between driving through an area at a speed which corresponds to our human structure and allows one, with many stops, to linger in an area with its special qualities, poetry, and reality, and, on the other hand, racing through an area, completely preoccupied by the destination one hopes to reach. It is the whole opposition between the principle of practical utility and the true, deep life, in which goods possessing a high value speak to us, where we truly live, where there is a present moment.

The airplane is certainly a great gift for mankind. In all situations where it is important to reach someone far away as fast as possible, it is, even from a purely human point of view, a priceless advantage. If a beloved person is mortally ill, it is possible, with the airplane, to reach his side while he is still alive. What an inconceivable gift! The airplane also affords many advantages from a cultural point of view. Great conductors, great violinists, and great actors can thus give joy to men in many places through their art.

And what an advantage to be able to reach by airplane distant lands which used to be accessible only to those who had unlimited time or who were sailors or naval doctors. Yet on the other hand, consider the "overdimensionalizing" of our human relationship to time, and the consequent spoiling of the experience of the reality of a completely different world, atmosphere, and culture. North America is a world in itself, completely different from the world of South America, and especially from that of Europe. We can no longer do justice to the richness of the world which is given through these different cultures if we have breakfast in New York and supper in Paris. The loss of the sense of the reality of one's surroundings which goes hand in hand with the "overdimensionalizing" of man's relationship to time and space is a very interesting problem. But we cannot go into all this here, for it does not belong specifically to the present theme, which is the illusion of progress. This problem belongs to a consideration of the "reverse side" of many positive advances, to an ecology of the spiritual-human realm.

Our theme is the radical decline and decadence of the human, spiritual, and cultural realm, an unprecedented disintegration, a dehumanization which no rational man can call progress unless he has closed his eyes and buried his head in the sand like an ostrich, or has repressed everything. It is sufficient for our purposes to show the apocalyptic process of dehumanization and the victory of collectivism and anarchy in our time. We therefore do not intend to go into the question of whether there is a relation between the advances which have a "reverse side," and this catastrophic, clearly negative process of human disintegration.

It is not difficult to see that the phrases, "adaptation of the Church to the modern age," impossibility of proclaiming the message of Christ to such an "advanced" era, in a word, *aggiornamento,* as the progressivists use this term, all have a different meaning, according to whether the present situation of the world represents true progress or terrible regress.

We have clearly shown in *The Trojan Horse,* as well as in *Celibacy,* that Divine Revelation, even in form, may not ever be changed to adapt it to the spirit of the age,[13] even if it really were an age of magnificent progress. But the enormous danger of mistaking regress for progress is nevertheless having disastrous consequences for the Church, as we shall see.

The present epoch is usually praised for the respect shown the human person, the dignity of man, and the freedom which he has achieved. But one sober glance at reality suffices to show that this is out of the question. For one thing, half of humanity is in the hands of the Communists. It is not necessary to prove that this means that the individual is enslaved in a way the world has never witnessed before. Present-day technology makes possible a degree of control over each individual person, over what he says and observes, and how he behaves in his private life, which the greatest tyrants of former times could not have enforced. All those in higher positions, moveover, who are not slave laborers, are even more enslaved spiritually; they are under continual supervision and are never out of the greatest danger. Only one loyalty still exists: loyalty to the state or party. Every other devotion, every other interest is already treason. A comparison with the very deplorable conditions of 150 years ago, in which serfdom certainly existed in Russia and China, and slavery in America, does not alter the fact that the disregard for the person and for human (as distinguished from political) rights has in one respect never reached such a degree as in the totalitarian states.[14] Here is the victory of collectivism, an utter devaluation of the individual, the likes of which the world has never seen before.

In addition to this is the continual "brainwashing," the use of mechanical means of persuasion, working through the mass media, the press, and education in the schools. This mechanical form of influence on the mind, effective by means of continual repetition, is indeed an unprecedented high point of disdain for personal dignity.

Unfortunately this decline in respect for the dignity of the person is not limited to the Communist countries. Even in democratic countries the victory of collectivism and the totalitarian spirit is asserting itself more and more. One need only reflect on the role of the mass media, and on the sub-

liminal kind of advertising which, though in itself less harmful than brainwashing, is nevertheless a mechanical form of
influence which bypasses the spiritual center of man and excludes a rational attitude. This kind of influence already contains in its formal structure an element of disdain for the
dignity of the person.

Here we must distinguish between two kinds of invasion
of the dignity of the person. On the one hand there is the
attitude of the state toward the individual person, the totalitarian invasion of the individual's most elementary human
rights. Secondly, there are currents among the general public
which are tolerated by the state and which include this disregard for the dignity of man. Let us turn our attention first
to the invasion of the totalitarian spirit in to the relations
between the state, the family, and the individual.

The legalization of abortion, which is slowly but surely
making headway, is indeed the most dangerous expression
of the disregard of the person. If one is allowed to take the
life of a human being, not as a punishment for a crime, but
from any consideration of practical utility whatever, then
respect for human life has been destroyed. In this connection
the words of Kierkegaard seem prophetic: "Our age proclaims as wisdom that which in reality is the mystery of
iniquity."[15] Man poses as lord over life and death. It is
forgotten that there is a world of difference between the
death penalty as punishment for a serious crime, and the
destruction of a human life for reasons of utility. If life can
be taken from a human being (and the child in the mother's
womb is unquestionably a human being) for any utilitarian
reason whatever, whether it be economic hardship or some
other reason for which the new person is not wanted, then
the way is clear for euthanasia carried out against the incur-

ably ill and the mentally ill (as Hitler introduced it and partially carried it out), and also for the killing of men past a certain age, when they are no longer "useful" to society. Man thereby becomes a thing which can be thrown away when it no longer functions properly.[16] This depersonalization, which no longer sees the inviolable value of the individual person in himself but which treats him like a thing is, in itself, a spiritual collapse. Of course, abortion is not yet compulsory; it is only permitted, and sometimes financially supported by the state. But this permission says much about the decline in respect for human life.

Another horrible totalitarian advance is the introduction of sex education in the schools. With this the rights of parents in regard to the education of their children are trampled underfoot, and that is a shocking totalitarian invasion. But much more despicable is the invasion of the soul of the child, to whom one presents a realm, which belongs to the specifically intimate sphere of human life, in a neutralized form in the public class room. It is a realm which is bound up with the "secret" of each person, to whose essence it belongs that one cannot objectify it and teach it like other subjects, such as languages, natural science, or mathematics. Each individual person has to discover this realm in his own special way. A certain veil must be drawn over this sphere and remain over it until the child reaches the level of maturity at which he can understand that this sphere is ordered in a special way to the unique, mutual self-donation of spousal love. The "scientific" instruction already being given to children from the age of six, which treats the sexual sphere as a purely biological matter to be handled in a prosaic, matter-of-fact manner, distorts this sphere and the right relationship to it.

The damage is not only enormous from a moral point of view, but also disastrous from a purely human viewpoint. The neutralization of the sexual realm which is already present in virtue of the publicity of the classroom, and especially in virtue of treating this realm as an academic subject, is dehumanizing. And it is a shocking totalitarian invasion on the part of the state.

One of the most deplorable consequences of this dehumanization (and here we turn to the second kind of dehumanization — the one embodied in prevalent attitudes) is the fact that the feeling of shame is dying out. In my book *In Defence of Purity,* I spoke of the various kinds of shame: shame about something ugly, shame about something intimate, shame about something good. We should be ashamed of our errors and sins. We should experience shame when someone praises our virtue and brings it out into the open, or when we ourselves make public things which are by their very nature intimate. All kinds of being ashamed are deeply human, classical attitudes, especially the shame which encourages us to keep intimate things out of the public eye.

It is a stupid mistake to interpret this latter kind of shame, which is especially related to the sexual sphere, as prudery, as contempt of this sphere, as a sign that one views it as tabu. It is certainly true that prudery and a negative attitude toward the sensual sphere are attitudes which have been widespread among certain people, especially in the Victorian era. But genuine, noble shame is a fundamental human attitude which is radically different from these aberrations. We may never judge the essence and value of a thing on the basis of the fact that there are also perversions and falsifications of it. Plato's comment remains true, that "the greatest evil is the hatred of reason," although rationalism is also a great evil. True and noble shame towards the sexual sphere, with which even the pagans were acquainted (just think of the gestures of the hands of many of the Venus figures, which covered the breasts and the pubic region), is a classical human characteristic, an adequate response to the mysterious intimacy of this sphere. A glance at the present suffices to bear witness to the unexampled shocking shamelessness in movies, the theater, on television, in the press, in advertisements for pornographic literature, and in many universities. Is this progress? Is it not rather a pitiful decline, a shocking sign of decay? Only a fool could, in the light of all this, still speak of the progress of our epoch. In comparison to this moral and human brutishness, what is the importance of the fact that man can now fly to the moon? Is man happier thereby? Or better on a human level?

A similar disrespect for the dignity of man is also present in the "sensitivity training" now being introduced in many places. Here one tries, through bodily contact, to create a community between men who do not know each other. This betrays an attempt from without to effect the mind mechanically by means of the body.

Social mores are also an important part of life. Of course, one should not overrate their importance, but they do have a legitimate place in the human sphere and their decline betrays an interior decay.

We need only think of the widespread outward disrespect of children for their parents, or of countless incidents such as that of a professor at an American university who was not fired, even though he spat in the dean's face during a disagreement, or of the student revolutions and their methods, or of the way in which some lawyers can berate and threaten judges with impunity! Just think of the political and public situation, where the kidnapping of innocent and uninvolved people is used as a pressure tactic to achieve a political goal, or of the hijacking of airplanes, endangering the lives of many totally innocent people. Or think of the lie of the United Nations, whose façade of justice and peace covers up the most infamous crimes, such as Biafra, or the expulsion of Taiwan from the U.N.; it pretends to be the unprejudiced last court of appeal, but at this court sit many who in principle do not acknowledge the principle of justice. When all this is seen, no rational man can overlook the fact that mankind is going downhill.

We have already spoken of the cowardice of those who make no use of their legitimate, God-willed authority.

One of the most doubtful phenomena of the alleged progress of our time is amoralism. There has always been immorality; men have committed sins from time immemorial. But the elimination of the fundamental categories of good and evil, which constitute the axis of the spiritual world, is a new development. This blindness to the fundamental reality of evil, reduces serious sins to something neutral (especially in the sexual realm, but in other areas as well) by interpreting them merely as psychologically interesting occurrences. In this, men believe themselves to be especially objective, because they have confused objectivity with neutrality.

And is the progressive disintegration of the family somehow to be considered "progress"? Is the increase of mental disease and suicide a symptom of how wonderfully far we have come? Ecology has already proved that technological advances have been bought at the price of weighty consequences for our biological existence and health. One of the things we need most today is a spiritual ecology which would demonstrate the disastrous consequences of so-called progress for man as a spiritual person, for his true human development.

Every unprejudiced glance at the state of culture in our time confirms the fact that we are now experiencing an enormous decay, a horrifying set-back, indeed, a disintegration.

I do not intend to go into the process of industrialization which began in the last century, around 1840. It cannot be denied that hand in hand with this industrialization went a loss of the sense of the poetry of nature and of life. It has brought the victory of utility, of comfort over beauty. The slowly increasing destruction of nature by railroads, telephone and electric lines, factories, advertisements of all kinds; the triumph of the machine and the mechanization of life which goes hand in hand with it: all this may be progress in civilization, but it is the ruin of culture.

And what can we say about architecture, which has produced no new and, more importantly, no beautiful style? The nineteenth century generated, for the most part, only poor imitations of the Gothic and other earlier styles. (This is in no sense to deny that great individual artists created magnificent individual edifices, especially fountains. Our concern here, however, is the decay of culture in the present era.) The so-called modern architecture is incomparably more catastrophic than the imitation characteristic of the nineteenth century. The anonymous, soulless, uniform rows of houses are a clear symptom of the dehumanization and desolation of a dull materialism. In order to see the decadence of modern architecture, we need only think of the tremendous treasure which has been produced in earlier times, of the magnificence of the architecture of the Greek temples in Paestum, of the Hagia Sophia, of San Marco in Venice, of Chartres Cathedral, of the Farnese Palace, of such baroque churches as Wies and Ottobeuren in Bavaria, or the Church of St. Charles in Vienna.

And what man with an artistic sense could not see the decline in the realm of art, whether in the plastic arts or in music? Where can one find in contemporary plastic arts and painting anything which can even remotely be compared with that of earlier times? Throughout all ages there have been incredible materpieces, from Egyptian and Greek antiquity through the period of the magnificent sculptures in the cathedrals of Bamberg, Chartres, and Rheims, and the statues of Donatello, Michelangelo, Bernini, and Schlueter. Even in the nineteenth century, extending up through the beginnings of the twentieth, there were great individual sculptors whose works are filled with genuine poetry. Whoever is not blind, however, sees the sorry state of the contemporary plastic arts, especially painting. How great is the painting of men like Cézanne, Renoir, van Gogh, Hans von Marées, let alone the glory of a Piero della Francesca, Giorgione, Tiziano, Rafael, Rubens, and Rembrandt.

And who can find anything in contemporary music which could be compared with Bach, Mozart, Beethoven, Schubert, Wagner, and Bruckner? When I speak of contemporary music, I am thinking above all of atonal music, and not of musicians such as Richard Strauss, Pfitzner, Braunfels, etc.

That which calls itself "art" today is largely an artificial, desperate attempt to create original things. But true beauty, poetry, and depth have disappeared,[17] except in the field of literature, where we still find true art today, as in the grandiose work of Solzhenitsyn.

Let us not forget what a source of happiness for man dries up when he lives in a world without poetry. To ascribe great importance to beauty as a source of happiness is not aestheticism, as many banal people claim. A psychiatrist, Dr. Bettelheim in Chicago, has even proved that beauty is very important for spiritual health. He uses reproductions of the paintings of great masters of the past in therapy with his patients. True beauty is thus not only a great and deep source of happiness, but also an important nourishment for the health of our souls.

And what are we to say about many of the philosophies which are widespread today? Symbolic logic, which is no true philosophy, offers no analysis of the great and truly philosophical problems. Heideggerianism, materialism, and many forms of relativism and immanentism are taught by ninety per cent of the philosophy professors in Europe and America — they should rather be called the undertakers of philosophy. This kind of "philosophizing" systematically destroys common sense, and with the incredible increase in the number of students a stupidity becomes widespread which above all ruins a healthy contact with life. But philosophy in itself is much more independent of the ruling tendencies of the age, of course, and there is still plenty of room for true philosophy.

What we have said may suffice to show how bizarre it is to regard our age as one of progress in comparison with former times, unless one limits oneself to the immanent progress in certain spheres such as natural science, technology, and, above all, medicine. But nobody can overlook the awful decay from a human viewpoint: the shocking depersonalization, the victory of collectivism, the progressive dehumanization, the decline of true happiness, and the sealing off of the true sources of happiness. What is the importance of immanent progress in certain areas in comparison with the decay of human life, with the moral, spiritual, and human deterioration of mankind?

This process is certainly not irreversible; it is not an inescapable fate. On the contrary, because man has a free will, this process can be arrested, thus clearing the way for a new ascent. But this ascent presupposes, in the first place, that we recognize the fantastic nonsense of regarding our era, taken as a whole, in essential and decisive points, as one of progress in comparison with earlier eras. The first step towards overcoming the decay, towards a new flourishing, is to recognize the entire seriousness of the situation, the apocalyptic character of our epoch.

Pope John XXIII said that the Church must leave her mark on every epoch and every land — and not *vice versa*. But what do we see today? *Aggiornamento* is interpreted to mean that the Church must be reformed in order to do justice to the great progress of our times, and to speak the right language to modern man, who has "come of age." Again and again, in sermons, pastoral letters, and lectures of "Catholic" theologians, we hear mention of progress. How enthusiastic was the response of even the highest levels in the Church to the technological progress making the flight to the moon possible, and how weak by comparison is the indignant disavowal of dehumanization. What is being done against the scandal of sex education in the schools? In many countries, the bishops themselves have introduced this criminal mutilation of children's souls into the Catholic schools. Where is collectivism clearly condemned? Can one find a syllabus such as that of the great Pius IX, in which present-day depersonalization in all areas, and the penetration of collectivism are unmasked and systematically opposed?

No, what we are seeing is not the struggle against the

Prince of this world who is present in so-called "progress"; not the attempt to imprint the Church's image on the age. We are witnessing the very opposite: the poison of our epoch is slowly seeping into the Church herself, and many have failed to recognize the apocalyptic decline of our time.

The wonderful treasurer of art and architecture — these documents of a truly Christian culture — have gone in large part unprotected and unpreserved. A kind of art which is not merely de-Christianized, but actually de-humanized is being proclaimed as "Christian" in churches which no longer possess any sacral character whatever. This is not to assert that the churches in the false Gothic style of the nineteenth century, or those which were unfortunate imitations of Romanesque, Byzantine, Renaissance, and Baroque churches, were adequate to their task. But they nevertheless testify to a well-meant, pious intention, even though the builders lacked a truly artistic talent. What we are experiencing today, on the other hand, is not, for the most part, the absence of artistic talent, but an intentional desacralization, a spirit of this-worldliness, a confusion of dull prose with holy simplicity. These things only give testimony to the penetration of the spirit of the age, with all its disastrous aspects, into the Church.

Instead of fighting against this spiritual decline, instead of giving support to the effort to conquer this apocalyptic decay, instead of letting the *lumen Christi* (light of Christ) shine forth without distortion, instead of holding fast to her glorious tradition, the Church is in too many instances letting herself be infected by this very spirit of the age.

One of the most hideous manifestations of dehumanization is artificial insemination. This belongs to the above-mentioned class of direct abuses, as distinguished from that negative "reverse side" of technological progress which is inevitable. We will limit ourselves here to a brief indication of the horror of artificial insemination, by pointing out the various awful disvalues which it contains.[18]

The first disvalue is the separation of the process of conception from the conjugal act. To disdain the great and very wonderful mystery of the creation of a new person being entrusted to this act, itself the expression and the unique fulfillment of spousal love, signifies a most sordid dehumanization. In various publications I have written much about marriage, about the divinely ordained role of the sensual sphere, and the conjugal act.[19] There is a deep and high value in the fact that the becoming one flesh of two lovers is the origin of a new person, and even in the fact that this mutual self-donation is linked to great bodily pleasure. This value is destroyed by artificial insemination. This is a dehumanization of the worst kind: the creation of a new person even sinks below the level of the animal world; it descends to the level of the artificial, technological sphere.

The second disvalue lies in the fact that the child has nothing more to do with the man whom the woman loves. It is the child of a stranger, an unknown person. A hideous depersonalization lies not only in the fact that the woman is thus in such intimate contact with a stranger that his sperm unites with her ovum, and that she carries this new, individual human creature under her heart, but also in the fact that the unknown man becomes a mere instrument, a mere bearer of sperm, whereby he descends to the level of an antibiotic which one injects to combat a disease.

Third, the wish for a child, which both loving parents have, is something beautiful, noble, and pleasing to God. But a woman's desire to have a child at any price, not necessarily the child of her husband whom she loves and who loves her, but a child as such, is already of a very doubtful nature. But when the wish to become pregnant and give life to a child goes so far that she accepts the injection of the sperm of a stranger in order to become pregnant, then it is definitely a perversion.

There is an abyss between the case of a childless married couple who adopt a strange child together, and the case in which a woman submits herself to an artificial insemination because her wish to bear a child is so isolated that she consents to such a hideous degradation. At bottom, this wish entails not only the break-up of marriage, but also the break-up of the family.

This accursed — and still relatively infrequent — practice reveals an increasingly widespread mentality which is preparing the complete suicide of all human dignity and true humanity. But above all, it is an abomination before God. We are thinking of the plans according to which the permission of the state would have to be obtained for the purpose of begetting children; that is, the begetting of children without the permission of the state would be forbidden. The reason given for this is the danger of overpopulation. But these plans in reality go far beyond this. For instance, there are plans for a bank in which sperm would be prepared with the most promising genes of specialists. This alone — by means of artificial insemination — would be allowed for women seeking to conceive.

This plan, which thank God is still only a plan, reveals clearly the terrible spirit which is spreading more and more, and which brings the realization of such plans completely within the realm of possibility.

Here diabolical dehumanization becomes plain for all to

see. First, artificial insemination, with all its horrible de-humanization, would be prescribed by law for all. That represents a totalitarian invasion into the intimate sphere of the life of the individual which even surpasses the totalitarianism of the Communists. Compared to this the Nazi regulation that an SS man was permitted to marry only a woman who was a certain number of centimeters shorter than he, was a harmless limitation of human freedom.

Secondly, in this plan everything is placed into the hands of "experts," who are thus assigned the role of Providence. In my book, *The New Tower of Babel,* I discussed this modern spiritual tendency: to want to play God. It is especially important to see how two apparently contradictory tendencies go hand in hand: on the one hand the trampling on the dignity of man, a depersonalization; on the other, the boundless presumption of men wanting to play God, to suppose they know how to do everything better than the Creator. These two phenomena go hand in hand because they both stem from man's denial of his metaphysical situation and his relation to God, and because man has forgotten or repressed his awareness of his creaturehood and of his true nobility as *imago Dei.*

Thirdly, this plan reveals a crass materialism. These "experts" are inspired by the nonsensical materialistic notion that the character, the spirit, the personality of man is causally determined through his genes and chromosones. Apart from the fact that much research into the relation between genes and the spiritual person still needs to be done, a fundamental error of all materialism also presents itself: the confounding of a causal relation in the sense of *causa efficiens,* with the relation by which one thing is a condition for the unhindered development of something else. Color, for example, can only be realized on an extended surface, or on an extended, material something, but extension itself does not produce or cause the color.

Similarly, a spiritual process such as an act of knowledge, presupposes a physiological, chemical process in the brain. If a man has received a blow on the head and lost consciousness for a time, he is not able to know or recognize anything while in this condition. But to maintain that therefore knowledge is a product of a chemical process, that it is a phenomenon which is causally determined by a chemical process, is obviously complete nonsense and leads to an absolute contradiction. If our knowledge were not, as it is, the spiritual capacity to ascertain something, if it were nothing but a psychic process which is produced by the chemistry of our brains, as a pain in my leg is produced by a physiological process in the nervous system, then I could never even know that there are chemical processes in the brain, nor anything about their relation to our spiritual life.

But the error of materialism is not our theme here.[20] In this plan, which reveals a great deal of terrible dehumanization, the whole idolization of science becomes plain. In a very unscientific manner this idolization places into the hands of science problems which are of a purely philosophical character and lie beyond the reach of any science. But the downfall threatening humanity lies especially in the fact that it is no longer a question of false theories only, but rather of their horrible penetration into our practical lives, leading indeed to the worst kind of totalitarian enslavement.

The threat is not only the destruction of human life by false theories which exercise their influence in a spiritual or intellectual way, such as the unfortunate influence of Freud's theories on our practical attitude towards the sensual sphere.

The false theories under discussion also have an influence on legislation and thus on the individual person when they lead to totalitarian violations of his private life and his inalienable human rights. What man with a modicum of understanding can here speak of progress? It is worse than a mere disintegration; it is truly a hell into which this "progress" is driving humanity.

One could object that it was claimed in the discussion of the myth of modern man that an epoch has no one uniform *Zeitgeist* which deeply moulds all the men of that epoch. But now that it is a matter of the illusion of progress, we do speak of a decline and a dehumanization of humanity.

This might admittedly appear contradictory at first glance, but if we look more closely, we see that this is not at all the case. We said before that the modern man, who has supposedly changed so much in his personality that he can no longer understand the language in which the holy Church has spoken to the individual for almost 2000 years, is an illusion, a myth. It may well be true that many false but fashionable philosophies present an obstacle to man's receptivity to the voice of the holy Church. But from that consideration we can only conclude that we cannot fight these false, fashionable philosophies enough. We must tirelessly refute them rationally, in order to eliminate them as obstacles. But we cannot at all conclude that the man who has been confused by these false, fashionable philosophies has thereby become another man, and that the proclamation of divine Truth must thus be adapted to him in a new form, as the religious instruction of a child must take a different form than that of an adult.

Moreover, it is not denied that there is a "spirit of the age," and that it takes many forms. It is expressed in the style and "feeling of life" of an epoch, as well as in the ideologies which, though they may predominate in one epoch, nevertheless by no means encompass all men living in this period. The decisive thing, however, is that the differences between individual men within one and the same epoch are much greater and deeper than the differences between humanity as it exists in different epochs.

Furthermore, this "modern man" who has come of age is presented as a proof of progress. He is supposed to be a specimen of something "higher," of a healthy, normal development. And with that we touch on the connection with the illusion of progress, for if there is no essentially new man, then the fact that the fictional modern man is treated as a higher state of evolution betrays the value blindness which is also characteristic of the general illusion of progress. Here a certain type of man is regarded as a normal development of man as such, and thus of humanity as a whole. It is believed that this "modern man," who in reality does not even exist, is superior and more valuable than the man of former times.

Our discussion of the deformation, the decline, the decay, and the dehumanization of the present world situation is not intended to reintroduce the concept of "modern man," but rather to unmask the terrible things which many people, unaware of their true nature, view as progress. We are not claiming that all men are deformed today, but rather that a deadly epidemic is widespread, threatening to infect countless men, and that some men, utilizing the enormous immanent advances of technology and natural science, are striving to produce an inhuman situation, a depersonalized and dehumanized world.

The recognition of the fact that an evil spirit rules the world to a large extent — this is of course a consequence of turning away from God — and is destroying the external freedom of man, his dignity, his true happiness, does not at all contradict our denial that a "modern" man exists as a consequence of a universal and essential change of the individual soul, which is moreover supposed to be the result of a normal evolution. The fact that today one half of humanity is in the hands of Communist dictators in no way proves that half of humanity is composed of Communists.

"Progress," and that tendency which theatens an unheard-of enslavement of mankind, and which in reality aims at a hellish dehumanization and depersonalization, is in no way an irresistible process. It is not a "fate," as represented by Karl Rahner in a lecture in St. Louis in 1970. We must here emphatically repeat what we stressed before when we were discussing the overall phenomenon of decay and apocalyptic dehumanization: all this horrible mechanization of life, playing God, the attempt by a group of "experts" to enslave every individual person, can be stopped if we struggle against it with all our strength. The clear recognition that the path we have trod leads into an abyss, can bring about a reversal, and a new flowering. Just as ecology fights against that destruction by technology of the external conditions of life, so a spiritual ecology must take up the battle against dehumanization. But we can only hope for victory through the conversion of individual men to God through Christ and to His holy Church. Only Christ can save mankind in this, perhaps its worst danger. The holy Church must take up the relentless battle against all plans for dehumanization and depersonalization.

But we must appeal to all men whose faculties of reason and common sense are still sound and natural, to join us in the battle. Our call extends to those truly cultivated men in whom there still lives a true ideal of humanity as opposed to those mere professors who are filled with intellectual pride.

In the lecture mentioned, Rahner declared that the Church takes a neutral position towards this development; she does not encourage it, but she does not fight it either. Thank God this is only Rahner's private assertion. There can be no question of a legitimate neutrality. But it is unfortunately true that the magnitude of this awful tendency is not seen clearly enough within the Church.

All the members of the "fifth column" within the Church, of whom I have already spoken, will naturally welcome this development. It fits in with their own efforts to destroy the holy Church. But all these people, whether they be laymen, priests, or bishops, in reality no longer belong to the holy Church, although they remain within the Church in order to reach their goal more effectively.

We have already mentioned that there are also many priests and bishops who do not belong to the "fifth column" at all, who are only blinded and overrun by these heresies, who want to swim with the times, who fear the judgment of the world more than they fear God. They are the ones who especially maintain that all the current, modern tendencies and developments are progress.

The situation is quite different with those who, in their desire to be positively attuned to the world and to do justice to the immanent progress in fields such as technology and medicine, do not recognize the magnitude of the decline, the true situation of humanity at the present moment. This circle in the Church will condemn the individual elements of decay, but they do not recognize the relation of these elements to the whole direction things are taking. Here we see an effect of the "this-worldliness" of which I will speak in greater detail later. This is, briefly, the emphasis on the improvement of the world, and on earthly progress in the sense of abolishing poverty, social injustice, and war, rather than on the salvation of the individual and the *glorificatio* of God; it is the emphasis on an earthly future rather than on eternity.

One hears a lot of drivel today about a new awareness of human qualities. One emphasizes that the Second Vatican Council has unmasked the dehumanization which has supposedly wrought havoc in the Church. But "awakened" man, who has come of age, is now supposedly restoring human values to their divinely ordained place in the Church.

But in reality the dehumanization of sinking down to the animal level is a specific sign of our times. Some of the very Catholics who accused the Church of dehumanization no longer want to be full, true men; their ideal is the animal. They let themselves be infected by the widespread fashion which presents a false image of full humanity, and which in reality represents a revolt against being an *imago Dei*. To see this, one need only read *The Human Ape,* in which this tendency is carried to its logical conclusions.[21] Here it is not a matter of men being governed by their animal instincts; there have always been men like this. Rather, it is a question of an idol which is being propagated by pseudo-intellectuals. It is a revolt against being the *imago Dei,* and a glorification of what is animalistic, wherein the animal is taken as a model.[22] This dehumanization goes hand in hand with a despiritualization. It is very indicative of the decline of culture and humanity that the sense of touch is placed in the foreground, ahead of the noble senses — sight and hearing. It is apparently assumed that the sense of touch mediates to us the reality of the world around us more than the eye and the ear. Therein lies a typical despiritualization, a descent to the animal level.

Although we in no sense want to minimize the great gift of *all* the senses, nor to deny the specific delight which the sense of touch conveys to us, still, the tremendous advantage and specific spirituality of sight and hearing must be pointed out.[23] Just let us think of the role of the eye, of sight, in our knowledge of the world around us, think of the distance to the object perceived with our eyes — of the distance to the object which is indispensable if we are to recognize it — of the spirituality of this sense. What a special role is played by sight in our relations with other people, and especially in art — architecture, painting, plastic arts — as well as in grasping the beauty of nature. The realm of the visible is an eminent "bearer" of beauty.

But think, too, of hearing: the ear possesses a spirituality analogous to that of the eye. Here also an analogous "distance" to the object can be found. Moreover, the audible is an eminent bearer of beauty. Just think of the realm of music! And what a role the hearing of words plays in the community of men! What meaning the hearing of their voices has! We need only think of the many-faceted role of speech in the spiritual contact with another person, and of all the poetry of the world of sounds.

It is a great error to believe that the sense of touch is more essential and plays a greater role in our knowledge of reality than the sense of sight. Of course, it conveys something which only it can convey, but to claim, as happens in sensitivity training groups, that the reality of another person is only fully grasped by us when we touch his body, is complete nonsense. The role of the sense of touch for human community is precisely one of expression, of an actualization, and in some cases, of a fulfillment of a bond which is already present. Shaking hands does not have the function of verifying the reality of the other person; rather it expresses our unity with him. The great and noble meaning of the kiss is only possible as an expression of an intimate bond; above all, a kiss on the lips and an embrace are a unique declaration of love. They not only presuppose a clear consciousness of the other person, but also a deep union of hearts — when they do not have a purely conventional character.

A typical symptom of despiritualization is contained in the present-day overemphasis of the sense of touch, in the attempt to ascribe a greater role to it than to sight and hearing. Perhaps one day we will give first place to the sense of smell — then we will truly have "gone to the dogs."

We have already elucidated in earlier writings, especially in the *New Tower of Babel*, and much earlier in *In Defence of Purity*, the essence of the intimate sphere, as well as the great role which it plays in the life of the person. But here we must once again examine the essence and fundamental meaning of intimacy, since the destruction of intimacy is gaining more and more ground today and represents a special form of depersonalization. It belongs to the essence of the human person here on earth that many things which he feels, especially his deep experiences, should not be exposed to public view. For example, in relationships with certain persons (relationships of deep love, of whatever kind) there is always something which resists the neutralizing, curious, seeing-from-without attitude of the "general public." The intimacy which is characteristic of every deep love in every category of love shields itself from neutral publicity, and indeed, from every violation by publicity, which is a desecration, and is radically opposed to the meaning and essence of this relationship.

It belongs to the full inner life of a person that he possesses an intimate sphere. This plays a central role both in his relation to God, in the *commerce intime* with Jesus — the most important and highest dimension of man — and in all deep relationships with other persons. The opening of our intimate sphere to another — in different measure, depending on the *logos* (specific nature) of the respective relationship — as well as our entrance into the intimate sphere of another, are essential components of deep relationships with other persons. When we say of a friend that we have come much closer to him, we mean precisely that we have become more intimate with him.

The highpoint of all intimacy within human relationships is found in spousal love and union. As we have discussed in other places (*In Defence of Purity*), the sexual or sensual sphere is the mystery of each person. It is specifically intimate and therefore the mutual disclosure of this mystery to the beloved is a unique fulfillment of the *intentio unionis*. Whenever one tries to strip the sexual sphere of its intimacy, one kills it; then the sexual union loses its character of a deep, mutual self-donation, and it is also robbed of all its deep charm. It is not difficult to see what a systematic battle is being waged against intimacy today, not only in the horrible sex education in the schools, but throughout man's personal life. This destruction goes hand in hand with the neutralization of this world and the elimination of its poetry. We repeat: without intimacy there is no true personal life.

Unfortunately, this destruction of intimacy has also penetrated the holy Church. The disastrous sex education introduced into many Catholic schools has been ordered by many bishops, and has not been strictly condemned and forbidden by Rome, at least not yet. The eruption of collectivism, of which we have already spoken and we will say more later, which has infiltrated into the liturgy under the title of the "communal," is hard to deny. One confuses thereby the earthly and heavenly "public realm," the supernatural community in Christ, with a bourgeois parish community, and the neighbor in the sense of love of neighbor (*der Nächste*) with neighbor in the sense of the person next door (*der Nachbar*).

Closely related to the destruction of intimacy is the systematic destruction of bashfulness. True bashfulness, also called *modestia,* and in English "modesty," is sharply opposed to all prudery; it is an essential component of authentic personality and belongs to true personal life.

It consists precisely in the fact that intimate things are experienced as intimate, and are withdrawn from the public eye. That man is coarse and superficial, "hollowed out" as a person, who never experiences shame, whether one praises his virtues publicly in his presence, or makes his vices known, or above all drags into the public his intimate life, his deep feelings and especially that which is connected with the sensual or sexual sphere. He also loses all his charm, everything mysterious about himself, and forfeits all personal depth.

There is of course the sheer perversion of exhibitionism, wherein a public display is made of sexual things. The shamelessness is, in this case, limited to the sexual sphere; it does not have a dull, neutralized, and depersonalized character, but rather that of something disgusting and embarrassing. But this shamelessness is not the specific danger which we are speaking of here; it is not more widespread today than in former times. The exhibitionist wants to show himself precisely to a stranger, because he is conscious of the intimate nature of the sexual sphere and finds a perverse satisfaction precisely in the exposition of the intimate, as well as in the shock which he brings about in the other person with whom he has no inner relationship whatever. No, we are thinking of the general shamelessness of the man who never experiences shame, of the dull man who discusses intimate things in public as though they were neutral matters, of the man for whom life and the world have become a "laboratory." He speaks about sexual things, even when they touch his own person, as one would talk in public about the weather; he neutralizes everything. This is the tendency of our time and an essential characteristic of depersonalization. How beautiful, how noble, how charming is the blushing of a young girl in certain situations!

It is inconceivable that so much of human life is being destroyed today under the title of "science." Even some bishops are completely blind to the catastrophe of depersonalization and the destruction of the natural sources of human happiness, reaching all the way to supernatural life. They see those who fight against this abomination as prudish, reactionary, merely clinging to what is customary, what they are used to.

It is truly incomprehensible how much one hears of the progress of our time in sermons, pastoral letters, Catholic books, etc. — how the belief in our enormous superiority over former times has penetrated the consciousness of Catholics. Are the signs of the times perhaps not clear enough? Do they not speak plainly enough? Indeed it is inconceivable that our hastening towards destruction is regarded as progress, right when we ought to be crying out: *"Inter vestibulum et altare plorabunt sacerdotes, ministri Domini et dicent: Parce, Domine, parce populo tuo!"* "Between the forecourts and the altar the priests and ministers of God will weep and they will cry out: Spare, O Lord, spare Thy people" (Joel 2:17).

NOTES

12. Medicine is the only area in which progress is of a completely positive nature, and in which disadvantages do not, as in other areas, necessarily accompany the advantages, that is, do not appear as the shadow unavoidably cast by the advantages. But even in the progress of medicine we encounter great dangers today.

13. Hence we read in the recent pronouncement (June 24, 1973) of the Sacred Congregation for the Doctrine of the Faith, an important document entitled "Declaration in Defense of Catholic Doctrine on the Church against Certain Errors of the Day": "It must be stated that the dogmatic formulas of the Church's Magisterium were from the very beginning suitable for communicating revealed truth, and that as they are now so they remain forever suitable for communicating this truth to those who interpret them correctly" (par. 5).

14. When we say that in one respect the disregard for the person in the totalitarian states has reached a high point never before seen in history, we in no way intend to deny all the terrible things which appear in the history of former times. The status of a Roman slave as a *res* (thing), a possession of his master, having no rights at all, the torture of later times, the slave trade in the United States up to 1863 — all this is certainly terrible, and manifests a radical disrespect for the person, his dignity and rights.

But the great difference is, first, that in those days it was a matter of a particular group of men, whether it was the "pariahs" (untouchables) in India, the slaves as opposed to the citizens of Rome, in later times serfs as opposed to freemen, the Blacks in North America as opposed to the Whites. The sin at stake here was to disregard the *equality* of men, who are all persons and are created in the image of God. The totalitarian states, on the other hand, do not (in principle) rob a particular group of men but rather all citizens of their human rights. The individual person is thus disregarded by the impersonal structure of the state.

In addition to this first decisive difference there is a second one. This collective theft of all rights of the individual person has much more scientific underpinnings and is more a matter of principle than the earlier slavery. It appears as an idol, as a result of progress, while the other was much less systematic, having more the character of a primitive egotism. It was a sign of primitive barbarity, whereas the totalitarian suffocation of the personal life is a terrible symptom of decadence, a refined disintegration. The same thing is true of physical tortures. The cruelty of the racking and burning of men issued from a primitive brutality, from a barbaric and bestial attitude. The cruelty of the totalitarian concentration camps is much more cunning, ingenious, and scientifically planned. It is not a symptom of a barbarian unawakedness, but rather the fruit of a fundamental blindness to the dignity of man. It is in relation to barbaric cruelty, as the cruelty of man is to that of a beast of prey.

Third, this totalitarian disregard reaches completely new depths. It is not limited to the torture of the body, but is primarily ordered toward the destruction of the mind and soul. Brainwashing strives to enslave man in his thoughts, in his ability to judge, in his free will; in short, to destroy the essential gifts of God which man has as *imago Dei*. It is a systematic spiritual castration carried out with all scientific means. And this castration is being presented as the way to the preparation of the earthly paradise (cf. *Brainwashed in Peking,* by Father van Coillie).

15. He said this at a time when the process of depersonalization and of amoral pragmatism, which is fully developed today, had just begun. Kierkegaard, *Point of View for My Work as an Author* (New York: Harper Torchbooks), p. 44.

16. In the case of euthanasia carried out against men who are no longer useful to the state, there is also the arrogant presumption that the state or some commission chosen by the state can decide whether the continued survival of a man may still be of value to the state and to the community. This is an incomparable level of decadence: for there is first the collectivist, totalitarian priority of utility over the right to life, and secondly the unheard-of presumption of granting a commission the competence to decide even on the question of utility.

17. The decay of contemporary art is especially shown by attempting artificial means for the realization of artistic beauty, in place of the unalterable means which God has entrusted to the senses. Also, men want to play God, and instead of inventing new things in the God-given ways, to substitute meaningless words for the true and only possible language. These "new" paths of art are not a natural, continuous development, or the result of weak talents, for there have always been mediocre and bad works of art. These are rather products of devilish pride, which seeks to replace God-given means by newly invented ones, to attempt invention where it is impossible.

18. We are excluding the case in which a doctor undertakes an operation, following the normal intercourse between a married couple, in order to convey the sperm more quickly to the womb, for this is quite a different matter. All our comments are directed toward the artificial insemination in which the sperm of another person is injected without any connection with the conjugal act.

19. *In Defence of Purity, Humanae Vitae: A Sign of Contradiction, Celibacy and the Crisis of Faith, Marriage, Man and Women.*

20. The true relation of body and soul has been investigated in a masterful way by Josef Seifert, in his book, *Leib und Seele (Body and Soul)*, which has just been published by A. Pustet Verlag, Salzburg.

21. Desmond Morris, *The Human Ape* (New York: Dell Publ., 1967).

22. C. S. Lewis aptly characterized this idol as "the trousered ape."

23. Hans Jonas has pointed out in a very beautiful way the unique nobility of sight in his essay, "Nobility of Sight."

5

Is There Still a Ray of Light?

GUARDINI, IN HIS BOOK *The End of the Modern Age,* commented on the decline of humanity and conceived of it as the downfall of Western culture. He saw it as an inevitable fate, as a process which we cannot stop. His main concern was how the Church will survive this collapse of mankind, in what form and manner.

But we would like to emphasize once again in the face of this apocalyptic decline of humanity that it is *not* an inevitable fate, that it can be avoided with God's help by the free intervention of those who see clearly that mankind is on the precipice, and that it is not, as the false prophet Teilhard de Chardin claimed, moving toward Christ the Omega Point in a magnificent process of evolution. It is high time that an ecology of the spiritual realm even on the natural level unmask this terrible error.

But above all, has Christ not redeemed mankind? Can He not halt this hastening toward the precipice by intervening in a way in which we cannot conceive of, but which we may hope for? And let us not forget how many magnificent things still do exist, that the message of God in the sun-filled heavens and in the beauty of nature still survives. Do we not, even today, still meet noble, pure persons, whose being radiates a light which makes us rejoice, men in whom a deep faith, a true love for Christ is alive? Indeed, are there not many saints even today?

No, the terrible decline of humanity, the whole, advancing dehumanization should certainly bring the gravity and seriousness of the situation before our eyes, but our response must not be despair, nor even discouragement, but rather a strengthened faith, an unconquerable hope, a stronger love — and the knowledge of the superhuman task of the holy Church: to save humanity — or at least her own children — from this downfall.

Is our life not a *status viae*, a state of pilgrimage? Is not hope the fundamental attitude which is characteristic of our *status viae?* The essence of the *status viae* is to be directed towards the point of arrival, the *status termini*, looking toward this with hope. This upward glance does not make us dull and indifferent to that which occurs in the *status viae*, and to our tasks and duties here. On the contrary, the prospect of eternity, for which we hope, grants us not only true wakefulness to take each moment of our lives seriously, but also the perspective of the true hierarchy of all natural goods. It is this view of things which protects us from viewing the horror of the present downfall as something final and inevitable; for the overwhelming reality of eternity gives us strength, courage, and hope to fight against this downfall.

And above all, we must pray that humanity, instead of hastening towards the precipice, return to true values. But this is only possible if the vineyard of the Lord blossoms anew. And therefore we must storm heaven with the prayer that the spirit of a St. Pius X might once again fill the hierarchy, that the great word *anathema sit* might once again ring out against all heretics and especially against all the members of the "fifth column" within the Church. *"Exsurge, quare obdormis, Domine; quare faciem tuam avertis, oblivisceris tribulationem nostram?"* ("Arise, why dost Thou sleep, O Lord? Why dost Thou turn Thy countenance from us and forget our tribulation?") Ps. 43, 23-25. Yes, let us urgently beseech God that the vineyard of the Lord be restored to its full glory — let us be filled with the hope which is expressed in the words of St. Anselm: *"In te, Domine, speravi: non confundar in aeternum!"* ("In Thee, O Lord, have I trusted: let me not be confounded in eternity!")

6

Is History the Source of Revelation?

IN MY BOOK, *The Trojan Horse in the City of God,* I spoke of the various ways of idolizing history, whether it be in the form of historical relativism or of a false interpretation of the "kairos." However, we intend here to turn our attention to the form which deifies history by claiming that Revelation did not stop with the Apostles, but that it continues through and in history. This error is unfortunately widespread today.

In it "salvation history" is no longer seen in its uniqueness, whereas profane history is placed on the same level as salvation history.

Of course this does not refer to the continuing formulation of the Divine Revelation handed down from the apostles, which goes hand in hand with the condemnation of heresies. This is the development from "implicit" to "explicit," which finds its expression in dogma, in the *depositum catholicae fidei,* the deposit of the Catholic faith. This development occurs under the protection of the Holy Spirit. But this clearly has nothing to do with the course of profane history, and is also no new revelation.

The claim that the supernatural revelation of God in the strict sense of the word still continues in history is also a failure to recognize the radical difference between the role of history in "salvation history" and in profane history. One does not notice the difference between that which is proper to history as such — or which is ascribed to it as such, such as the imaginary Hegelian World-Spirit — and unique, supernatural intervention at a particular moment in history.

The Holy Father gave a clear answer to this question in an audience on January 19, 1972:

"The question is this: is the contact with God which issues from the Gospel a moment which belongs to the natural development of the human spirit, and is thus subject to continual change and to being continually surpassed? Or is it a unique and decisive moment on which we can nourish ourselves without ceasing, wherein we nevertheless recognize the essential content to be unchangeable? The answer is clear: this moment is unique and decisive. That means that Revelation has entered time and history; it is a precise datum, tied to a particular event, which must be considered as finished and — for us — completed with the death of the Apostles (cf. Denzinger-Sch. 3421). Revelation is a fact, an event, but at the same time a mystery which does not spring from the human spirit, but from divine initiative, which was progressively manifested in the course of history throughout the Old Testament, and which reached its highpoint in Jesus Christ" (cf. Heb. 1:1; I John 1:2-3; Constitution *Dei Verbum,* Nr. 1).[24]

The Church distinguishes unambiguously and clearly between this unique Revelation of Christ, which is finished with the death of the last Apostle, and all private revelations, even when these are recognized as genuine and are distinguished from all pretended or ungenuine private revelations. But these private revelations never refer to dogmatic questions of faith and morals, as does Christian Revelation. Many saints and mystics have had visions and dialogues with Christ, for example, St. Gertrude, St. Teresa of Avila, St. Catherine of Siena, St. Francis of Assisi, and St. John of the Cross. But all these refer to unique experiences, to the relationship between the saint and Jesus, or to concrete instructions — but all within the framework of the official *depositum catholicae fidei*. If anything occurred in these private revelations which contradicted the *depositum catholicae fidei,* the saintly mystics themselves viewed it as a deception. But there is no obligation for the Catholic believer to include the content of these private revelations in his faith.[25]

Moreover, there are supernatural appearances, such as in Lourdes or Fatima, which are clearly distinguished from all Revelation of God in Christ, for this ended with the Apostles. They are great miracles — in part miraculous healings, in part supernatural warnings — but they represent no additions whatever to Revelation in the strict sense of the word, which terminated with the Apostles. The latter apparitions are not private apparitions, as in the case of the holy mystics, for their messages were directed to all. The persons who experience them have more the character of a mouthpiece: in Guadalupe, it is a simple Indian, who had no other visions or mystical experiences; in Lourdes, a very young girl, Bernadette; in Fatima, children who, while they did become saints, were not typical mystics. Here again it is not a matter of revelation in the sense of divine revelation of the content of faith and morals, as is the Revelation laid down in the *depositum catholicae fidei.*

But many progressivists view history as revelation in the full sense, as an enlargement and continuation of the Revelation of God in Christ through the Apostles. There is talk especially of the revelation through the Holy Spirit in history. This is decidedly false, and expressly marked by the Holy Father as an error.

But, it could be objected, the old saying, *"vox temporis — vox Dei"* ("the voice of the times is the voice of God") has real meaning, and can in no way be interpreted as an expression of modern historicism. This saying gives clear expression to the fact that God speaks to us in history, and indeed in the present moment in history. The present epoch thus contains a message from God to men, and this message must be understood and assimilated. We must follow the call which lies in this message. To be deaf to this message — so they think — would be very wrong; it would be disobedience to God.

This may sound plausible to many people. But as soon as the true meaning of *vox temporis — vox Dei* is more carefully analyzed, it becomes quite clear that it means something completely different than what is meant by the slogan that "God reveals Himself in history," in the sense discussed above. The *vox Dei* refers to special tasks which are assigned to us — but in no way to Divine Revelation. Of course the particular age in which we live makes special requirements of us. When orders were founded in the Middle Ages to free the Christians who had been captured by the Moslems, special historical circumstances contained a call of God to such an undertaking. The splendid relief work done by Father Werenfried van Straaten, the so-called "bacon-priest," is a typical response to the awful spiritual and physical need into which many have been thrust by the great evil of Communism.[26] The appeal of God for this relief work did not exist one hundred years ago.

Each age poses problems which previously had not existed. But the new problems are not posed by the "spirit of the age," but rather by new facts. The solution of these problems, however, should never come from the "spirit of the age" but from the spirit of Christ. The "spirit of the age" in the sense of the prevailing ideology, only sets the task of combatting the errors which were formerly not influential. Certainly the encouragement of whatever good is to be found in the spirit of the age is a divinely ordained task. But all this clearly has nothing to do with a revelation of God in the sense of the disclosure of the divine mysteries. There is no question of new truths of faith, but a call to fulfill certain tasks which are presented by the respective era. The *vox Dei* in a particular age is not revelation in the strict sense of the word. It has no supernatural character.

An era also does not teach us principles with regard to moral questions. We are confronted with new tasks in a particular historical situation; the call of God here is to fulfill them. But the epoch does not instruct us about good and evil. God often calls us precisely to resist all false teachings which present themselves as Christian, according to the words of St. Paul: "For the time will come when they will not stand wholesome teaching, but will follow their own fancy and gather a crowd of teachers to tickle their ears. They will stop their ears to the truth and turn to mythology" (2 Tm. 4: 3-4).

The radical difference between that which is meaningfully expressed by the saying *vox temporis* — *vox Dei*, and Divine Revelation, can be seen clearly when we compare profane history with salvation history. The salvation history in the Old Testament contains revelations in the full sense of the word. The Revelation of God, whether it be to Abraham or through Moses and the prophets, is a divine intervention at a particular historical moment. This is incomparably more true of the self-revelation of God in Christ. All the deeds of Christ take place in history. But this direct intervention of God in history is separated by an abyss from that which profane history can tell us about God. And especially all the words of Christ are a revelation which took place in history at a particular moment, but which themselves, as such, go *completely* above and beyond salvation *history.*

NOTES

24. Address of Pope Paul VI to the general audience of January 19, 1972, *Osservatore Romano,* English Edition, Jan. 26, 1972.

25. It suffices if he deeply venerates the holy mystics and if possible asks for their intercession, and treats reverently the private revelation as a great gift of God to the saint. This is what is required, but this is not to say that express concern with these private revelations cannot be a source of edification and help in one's spiritual life. Indeed, the fact that there is such a thing as this direct supernatural relation of the saintly mystics to Christ, should fill us with joy. To be edified by this belongs indeed to the fully religious life of every truly believing Catholic.

26. This great project began right after World War II, originally also as a help for starving Germany. Today it extends to the "third world," but especially to Communist-dominated countries.

7

"Qui te fecit sine te..."

A DANGEROUS ERROR, which has unfortunately also penetrated into the sanctuary of the Church, is the notion of progress, unfolding in history, in our objective relation to God, wherein it is assumed that God is drawing mankind closer to Himself in the course of history without the individual knowing anything about it. This is especially a fruit of Teilhardism.

It is very important to understand that no man can attain eternal beatitude without his own cooperation.[27] *"Qui te fecit sine te, non te justificat sine te,"* says St. Augustine.[28] ("He who created you without you does not justify you without you.") Even though the cooperation of the individual is only a tiny factor in comparison with the infinite mercy of God — the redemption through Christ's death on the cross, the reception of sanctifying grace at baptism — nevertheless, this cooperation with grace — obedience to the commandments of God, faith, hope, love, the imitation of Christ — is a factor of decisive importance.

The Gospel leaves no room for doubt that God treats man as a partner, and that our behavior, our response plays a decisive role in our sanctification, and through it, in the glorification of God, and finally in our eternal beatitude. Christ said, "Truly, I say unto you, if your justice is not greater than that of the Scribes and Pharisees, you will not enter the Kingdom of Heaven." Further, "Not everyone who says to me, 'Lord, Lord,' will enter the Kingdom of Heaven, but those who do the will of my Father, who is in heaven."

It is obviously impossible to enumerate all the passages in the Gospels which point out the importance of our obedience to the commandments of God and of our love of God and neighbor. This is indeed the meaning and essence of Revelation: that God speaks to us as persons, and as persons we thereby become acquainted with supernatural truth and give the response which God wishes us to give to this truth: our faith. It also belongs to the meaning of Revelation that we become acquainted with the commandments of God and obey them. It belongs to the meaning of the Revelation in the God-Man Jesus Christ that His adorable holiness shine resplendent upon us, and that we follow and imitate Him. Faith, hope, and love should blossom in us and that requires — apart from the gift of grace, the communication of the divine principle of life in baptism — our free cooperation. We do not, therefore, reach eternal beatitude without having anything to do with it. When we think of all other creatures, such as plants and animals, we realize that everything happens to and through them without their free cooperation. They are not personal creatures; a revelation to them would have no point. They possess neither the capacity for true knowledge and true understanding, which belongs to man alone, as a person, nor do they have a free will.

Now it is important to understand which things even in human life issue from God alone, without man's cooperation, and which things require free cooperation. *"Qui fecit te sine te,"* says St. Augustine. That we exist, our life as persons, that we possess the capacity for knowledge and freedom of will: all these are pure gifts of God, which we receive. Here it would have no meaning to speak of our cooperation. The action of Providence in our lives is also completely independent of us. When a person thinks of all the circumstances of his life, of all the situations into which he has been led without having had a hand in the matter, he catches a glimpse of an enormous network of things which came into being without his assistance: which parents he had, which brothers and sisters, in which environment he was allowed to grow up, how he is physically put together, whether he is infected during an epidemic or not, whether he meets persons of whom he had previously known nothing, but who afterwards play a decisive role in his life. In the entire dominion of Providence we are dealing with pure dispensations of God, in which no cooperation is present on our part, and which are forthcoming without our playing a conscious part in them. The special graces which God gives the individual person are also pure gifts.

It is impossible to treat in detail here everything in our lives which is a pure gift of God, in the sense that it presents itself without our knowledge and without our cooperation. There would naturally be many levels to distinguish here. There are for instance many things which lie completely beyond our power, which in principle occur without our having anything to do with their occurring and others, which in principle can come about through our cooperation (for example, the encounter with other persons, as when one expressly seeks someone whom one has heard of). We could also distinguish the things which, though they are pure gifts, still come into our experience, such as the inspirations of an artist, a great love for a particular person, the grace to feel the presence of God, to experience a burning, ardent love for Christ. These are all gifts, but not things which happen without our having anything to do with their coming to us. And besides these there are many gifts which appeal to us for a right response.

The main distinction is perhaps here: which things occur without our having anything to do with their occurring, which only intrude into our conscious life when they are fully real? Consider, for example, a sickness which develops for a long time unnoticed, or numerous occurrences in our bodies. Everything which invades our consciousness, though it take place without us and our cooperation, is nevertheless known by us, addresses itself to our consciousness and, what is more, appeals to us for a response. But we cannot go into further detail here concerning this problem, which is most interesting in itself. For us the decisive fact is that there is no morality without our free cooperation, and that nobody can partake of eternal beatitude without his own cooperation; and indeed, that the Revelation of God must be heard and grasped, that it addresses itself to our consciousness and is an appeal for our cooperation — a cooperation which is required for sanctity and eternal beatitude, which brings "fear and trembling" over us.

The notion that in the course of history humanity is being drawn nearer to God by "progress" in history is based on a Hegelian error which we discussed in detail in *The Trojan Horse*: we are never drawn nearer to God without our having anything to do with it, and without our noticing it.

Every instance of being drawn nearer to God is something which can only have reference to the individual; it may refer to many individuals at the same time, but never to humanity, or to a community. Here, too, we encounter the Hegelian error of depersonalization, of the primacy of the community over the individual person, which leads him, for example, to regard the state as a higher entity than the individual person.

Here an especially dangerous invasion of Hegelian historicism presents itself: the notion that being drawn nearer to God takes place through the alleged progress in history, "over our head," as it were.

NOTES

27. Obviously I am thinking here of adults, who have the use of reason and of their free will. A small child, in whom this is not yet present, can certainly participate in eternal beatitude without his cooperation if he is baptized.

28. St. Augustine: Sermones (de Script. N.T.) CLXIX, XI, 13.

8
The Great Disappointment

AT THE SECOND VATICAN COUNCIL there was much discussion, full of hope, of a great renewal of religion, which would be deepened and divested of any purely conventional accretions. But if someone were to regard with an unprejudiced mind the Church of today, and compare it with the Church of 1956, what would strike him? Changes, surely, but he would search in vain for renewal and deepening of faith in the Revelation of Christ, as it is laid down in the *depositum catholicae fidei* (deposit of the Catholic faith), and for a more vital life in Christ, a more living imitation of Christ.

Nuns who formerly even by their habits radiated a life completely consecrated to God, and withdrawn from all that is worldly, now confront us in make-up and miniskirts.[29] In many places the Holy Mass is celebrated with jazz and with all kinds of rock and roll music. But even in many churches where the Holy Mass is correctly celebrated, we see the

66

faithful standing to receive Holy Communion. Why, one asks oneself, has kneeling been replaced by standing? Is not kneeling the classical expression of adoration? It is in no way limited to being the noble expression of petition, of supplication; it is also the typical expression of reverent submission, of subordination, of looking upwards, and above all it is the expression of humble confrontation with the absolute Lord: adoration. Chesterton said that man does not realize how great he is on his knees. Indeed man is never more beautiful than in the humble attitude of kneeling, turned towards God. So why replace this by standing? Should kneeling perhaps be prohibited because it evokes associations with feudal times, because it is no longer fitting for "democratic" modern man? Does religious renewal perhaps consist in becoming a victim to purely associative thinking (a clear sign of stupidity)? Does religious renewal lie in suffering from an unfortunate case of "sociologitis," which nonsensically wants to deduce fundamental human phenomena from a particular historical epoch and kind of mentality? And why can the faithful no longer kneel beside one another at the Communion rail — which is after all a great expression of community — why must they march up to the altar goosestep fashion? Is this supposed to correspond to the meal character of Holy Communion (which is stressed so frequently) better than kneeling together in a recollected way? [30]

Unfortunately, in many places Communion is distributed in the hand. To what extent is this supposed to be a renewal and a deepening of the reception of Holy Communion? Is the trembling reverence with which we receive this incomprehensible gift perhaps increased by receiving it in our unconsecrated hands, rather than from the consecrated hand of the priest?

It is not difficult to see that the danger of parts of the consecrated host falling to the ground is incomparably increased, and the danger of desecrating it or indeed of horrible blasphemy is very great. And what in the world is supposed to be gained by all this? The claim that the contact with the hand makes the Host more real is certainly pure nonsense.[31] For the theme here is not the reality of the matter of the Host, but rather the consciousness, which is only attainable by faith, that the Host in reality has become the Body of Christ. The reverent reception of the Body of Christ on our tongues from the consecrated hand of the priest is much more conducive to the strengthening of this consciousness than reception with our own unconsecrated hands. *"Visus, tactus, gustus in te fallitur, sed auditu solo tuto creditur,"* says St. Thomas Aquinas in his magnificent hymn, *Adoro te.* ("Sight, touch, and taste would err about Thee; but through hearing alone are we given certain faith.")

Or is it perhaps the crude error that through an imitation of the external customs of the first Christians we could regain the faith of these Christians? These customs were good at that time because an unshakeable, heroic faith was present, a faith which confessed Christ at the risk of death. Certain forms were possible at a time when the opposition between sacred and profane was so lively, at the time of the catacombs when reverence was so great. But the simple reintroduction of these forms could never rejuvenate the faith of a conventional or modernistic Catholic, or make him more reverent.

But, many will object, the character of the meal is thereby strengthened. But is Holy Communion the moment to play-act and to imitate a meal — which is a holy meal, and in any case completely different from a real meal — rather than to focus on the unspeakable mystery of the love-union of our souls with Jesus, and through this, with all the faithful? And the real imitation of a meal which takes the form of a breakfast is a blasphemy, as every rational man must see. It is, thank God, not yet officially permitted, but unfortunately it occurs over and over again. Incidentally, Communion in the hand is permitted in many countries, but is in no way recommended by Rome.

Much more serious yet is the unfortunate mutilation of the liturgical year and the Holy Mass in the New Ordo. Is our faith supposed to be renewed and vivified by greatly weakening our sense of community with Christians of former times, a community which is so centrally important for the true Christian ethos? Is it perhaps believed that the community with the living, with contemporaries, becomes stronger by weakening the community with the saints of former times? Quite the opposite is true. The Christian community, the supernatural community is necessarily extended into the present and the past.[32] This is precisely a particular characteristic of this supernatural community which distinguishes it from all purely natural and humanitarian kinds of community. The real, experienced union with the saints of former times is a specific manifestation of true faith, a breakthrough to valid, supernatural reality. It found its glorious expression in the celebration of the feasts of the saints, in which the saint of the day was not only mentioned in the Collect and Postcommunion, as is now the case, but in which his figure was luminously prominent in the wonderful construction of the whole Holy Mass: in the text of the Introit and the Gradual, in the choice of the Epistle and the Gospel. Let us think, for example, of the feasts of St. Francis of Assisi, St. Martin, St. Agnes, St. Andrew, and above all of the feast of the Conversion of St. Paul, the feast of Saints Peter and

Paul, in order to see that the liturgy knew how to bring us completely into an intimate union with these individual saints. And let us think of the role of the saints in the Tridentine Confiteor and Canon. One accused oneself before God, the Blessed Virgin, and the whole heavenly court. One was conscious of deep community with them; one made this self-accusation before God in the supernatural world, in which alone one can be simultaneously sheltered in an intimate and personal way, and present in a holy public realm. Some of this has disappeared; some has been placed completely in the background in favor of an emphasis on the more or less accidental parish community.

The new liturgy was simply not formed by saints, *homines religiosi,* and artistically gifted men, but has been worked out by so-called experts, who are not at all aware that in our time there is a lack of talent for such things. Today is a time of incredible talent for technology and medical research, but not for the organic shaping of the expression of the religious world. We live in a world without poetry, and this means that one should approach the treasures handed on from more fortunate times with twice as much reverence, and not with the illusion that we can do it better ourselves.

The so-called "renewal" of the liturgy has robbed us of any possibility of a true participation in the liturgical year. In the Tridentine Mass one experienced in a living way Advent, Christmas, Epiphany, Septuagesima, Lent and Passion Week, the Resurrection of Christ, the glorious Easter season, the Ascension of Christ, the anticipation of the Holy Spirit, and the blissful feast of Pentecost. How significant was each part in the structure of the Mass: the Introit, the Epistle, the Gospel of the feast which was being celebrated! What a role the *celebration* of the feasts played! The entire, deeply meaningful dimension of celebration fostered true community in Christ, in which all have a share in the holy joy: *"Gaudeamus omnes in Domino diem festum celebrantes."* ("Let us all rejoice who celebrate this festive day in the Lord.")

With the disappearance of the celebration, we find that listening has disappeared. This holy stillness within our souls, however, is necessary in order to let the word of God radiate into our souls, and then to let us participate in the inconceivable mystery of the Sacrifice of Christ, and afterwards, to receive into ourselves Jesus, our Lord and our Beatitude.

The new liturgy is without splendor, flattened, and undifferentiated. It no longer draws us into the true experience of the liturgical year; we are deprived of this experience through the catastrophic elimination of the hierarchy of feasts, octaves, many great feasts of saints, and through the practice, in the remaining feasts of saints, of remembering the saint only in the Collect and Postcommunion.

Truly, if one of the devils in C. S. Lewis' *The Screwtape Letters* had been entrusted with the ruin of the liturgy, he could not have done it better. In place of the deep expression which even makes use of our bodily postures — sitting for the Epistle and the offertory, standing for the Gloria, the Gospel, the Credo, and kneeling in adoration — we now have a continual up and down which works against recollection.

What was the idea behind lengthening the Liturgy of the Word (the Mass of the Catechumens) on Sunday and in many instances also on weekdays, and shortening the actual *sacrificium?* What a mistake to believe that in the "instructive" part a larger portion of the Old Testament must be read and that all four Gospels must be proclaimed one right after the other. Is not the function of the reading and of the Gospel in the Holy Mass a completely different one from merely publicizing the Old and New Testaments? The reading of the Bible cannot be recommended enough; Bible-study evenings, where the priest and the faithful read texts from the Old and the whole of the New Testament, would certainly help bring about more intimate knowledge of the Word of God. But in the Holy Mass, whose focal point is the Holy Sacrifice, through which God is infinitely glorified, together with Holy Communion, the reading and the proclamation of the Gospel do not have an instructive function, but rather serve the spiritual preparation of our souls for the Sacrifice and Communion. The attitude which is fitting here for these readings is not that of learning, but that of reverently letting the light of Revelation shine upon us, especially such parts of it as have a special relation to the feast which is being celebrated. The unique character of the feast, be it Christmas, Epiphany, the Ascension, or the Immaculate Conception of Mary, is closely bound to the choice of the readings, be they from the Old Testament or from the letters of the Apostles, or from the Gospels. Instead of this, the organic structure of the feasts is destroyed, and replaced by the mechanical principle of having the Gospels of Matthew, Mark, Luke, and John follow each other in sequence, so that in the course of three years all four Gospels will be read in their entirety.

The universal Latin, which throughout so many ages was the sacral language of the Roman Catholic Church, has been replaced by the vernacular,[33] and the quality of the vernacular translations have rendered it more difficult to be drawn into the sacral world of the supernatural, and have confined us within a banal world. And what should be said of the *de facto* abolition of Gregorian chant,[34] this glorious, timeless voice of the Church, which has almost the character of a "sacramental"?

Have all these changes served the renewal and vivification of faith? The opposite is the case. Vocations to the priesthood, as well as conversions, have greatly decreased, and attendance of Catholics at Mass has greatly fallen off. The new *Ordo Missae* and most especially the reform of the liturgy of the feasts and of the whole liturgical year, is so colorless, inorganic, and artificial, that it will not be able to last long. What a sacred world was radiated in the organic structure and beauty of both the Tridentine Mass (which had already been used in its essential elements long before its official introduction), and the structuring of the feast days: the feasts of our Lord, of the Mother of God, of the great, special feasts of the saints, and even of the *commune sanctorum!* This was all especially beautiful in combination with Gregorian Chant. Present in this liturgy was thus a vitality and a power to live, so that throughout all the centuries it lost none of its surprising depth and beauty. But these things disappear in the new liturgy. We are therefore justified in hoping that this liturgy will be short-lived. Indeed, its failure from a pastoral viewpoint is a further sign that we are justified in this hope. So we can expect that the Church in the foreseeable future will return to the glorious Mass of St. Pius V and the magnificent arrangement of the whole liturgical year in all the changeable parts of the Holy Mass.

But despite the grave defects of the new Mass, it would of course be completely wrong in any way to question its validity as a reenactment of the sacrifice of Calvary, as unfortunately some few orthodox Catholics have. And it goes without saying that it would also be completely wrong to disobey any of the rulings of the Holy Father regarding the *Novus Ordo* and the Tridentine liturgy (cf. the passage from Vatican I quoted in footnote 78-a, regarding the obedience which Catholics owe the Pope even in those practical matters where they are entitled to disagree with the judgment of the Pope).

Turning to a different subject: promiscuity, even among Catholics, has increased in a horrifying manner. Certain Catholic universities, as mentioned above, have even become places of shameless public indecency, and many of their professors, both priests and religious, not only teach things which are completely incompatible with the dogmatic teaching of the Church, but also defend promiscuity. Where is the promised renewal?

We have to consider yet another respect in which the hope of renewal has been disappointed. Many had hoped that through the Second Vatican Council a conquest of mediocrity would go hand in hand with the freeing of the religious life from all merely conventional elements. Were not many bishops, and especially many priests and pastors, mediocre? It was believed that this mediocrity was due to the narrowness of the seminaries, to isolation from the world — in a word, to the fact that the Church had withdrawn into a ghetto.

But with what success have we burst out of our so-called narrowness? What we encounter in theological books, essays, and sermons is not only a spirit of irreverence, and of apostasy, but also a deeply oppressive mediocrity. Mediocrity is well known to be more fatal, the more the mediocre person believes himself to be intelligent, interesting, novel — the more he regards "revolutionary" and "mediocre" as radical opposites. Certainly there have always been mediocre bishops, priests, and theologians in the history of the Church. They were not *"homines religiosi"*; they did not radiate the spirit

of the holy Church in their personalities. They were intellectually insignificant, and when they wrote books or gave
sermons, their manner of presenting the sublime teaching
of the holy Church was mediocre, even if well-intentioned.
But their sermons, pastoral letters, and books contained no
heresies — and if they did contain them, they were immediately disavowed by the higher authorities. Thus even
these mediocre figures in the Church remained spokesmen
for the Church and her true teaching.

But the mediocrity which is devastating the vineyard of
the Lord today does not only refer to personality, but also to
the content of what is being propagated. Since many are
no longer functioning objectively as spokesmen for the
teachings of the holy Church (although they pass themselves
off as such), but rather proclaim the fruits of their own
thought in place of the *depositum catholicae fidei,* the content of their teaching is also filled with mediocrity. The
fact that they are allowed to do this unhindered signifies a
triumph of mediocrity within the Church which formerly did
not exist.

A cancerous damage is being caused by the whole program
of renewal because it deliberately builds on experimentation.
The childish, primitive idolization of science has awakened
in many the notion that one should ascertain even in the
pastoral realm, by conducting experiments, what has stronger
effects, what attracts people, etc. But the experiment, which
is so completely appropriate in the realm of natural science,
is not fruitful, nor even possible, in philosophy, and especially not in our practical life. One cannot make experiments
with souls; one cannot make experiments in the pastoral
realm. The proclamation of the Revelation of Christ cannot
be changed in order to ascertain by experiment what is more

"attractive." The pastoral sphere cannot be separated from the nature of the content of Revelation — nor from the essence of the human soul; it cannot be separated from that which it *should* be. It must never be made into a purely psychological concern. The experimental, neutral attitude is incompatible with the pastoral attitude. The ultimate seriousness with which the immortal soul is taken in every true apostolate is the opposite of the neutral attitude towards an object which one experiments with. This wretched idolatry of the experiment has penetrated deeply into the Church. It has affected those in positions of authority less in what they recommend than in what they permit. The slogan of experimentation is the key to get permission to undertake everything imaginable. The "experimental" frame of mind nourishes the illusion that one is "renewing" the Church, that one is freeing oneself from all conventionalization of faith — although this attitude is from the outset incompatible with all true religious attitudes and is itself much worse than all conventionalization, which is of course regrettable.

Let us think of the genuine renewal and the true blossoming of faith and of Catholic life which developed in France at the beginning of the century, at the time of Léon Bloy, Claudel, Péguy, Jammes, Maritain, Psichari and many others — of the religious flourishing even in the working class, of the time when Pope St. Pius X called forth a true renewal of the liturgy through an encyclical and through his glorious war against Modernism; then it can only sound ironic to speak of the renewal, deepening, revitalization of faith and of Christian life through Vatican II. Though there may well have been many things in need of reform before the Council, a comparison of the Church in the year 1956 and in 1972 compels one to say with the Psalmist, *"Super flumina*

Babylonis illic sedimus et flevimus cum recordaremur Sion." "By the rivers of Babylon we sat and wept, when we remembered Sion" (Psalm 136).

NOTES

29. Fortunately Rome has given more concrete directives in the meantime regarding the dress of religious, with the intent of remedying such abuses.

30. Prof. Ferdinand Holboeck of Salzburg gave a striking sermon on kneeling, which later appeared in Salzburg as an essay, *Beuget die Knie.*

31. In the propaganda for Communion in the hand we encounter an overemphasis on the sense of touch; and, as we saw above, this goes together with the despiritualization of man. But not even this overemphasis is an argument for Communion in the hand; for, the sense of touch also plays a role when the Host is received on the tongue. The hands are, after all, not the only bodily organs which give us sensations of touch.

32. It is a regrettable and serious symptom that, although the priest may choose which of the four Canons (Eucharistic Prayers) he will use, the Roman Canon (now named Number 1) is so seldom read, even by completely orthodox priests. See especially the concluding chapter of this book: How God Wants Us to Respond in the Present Crisis.

33. But this is contrary to the express intent of the Council: "Particular law remaining in force, the use of the Latin language is to be retained in the Latin rites" (*Constitution on the Sacred Liturgy,* no. 36, par. 1). And after allowing a limited use of the vernacular in the liturgy, the Council says: "Nevertheless steps should be taken so that the faithful may also be able to say or to sing together in Latin those parts of the Ordinary of the Mass which pertain to them" (*ibid.,* 54).

34. The *Constitution on the Sacred Liturgy* says: "The Church acknowledges Gregorian chant as proper to the Roman liturgy; therefore, other things being equal, it should be given pride of place in liturgical services" (no. 116).

9

Change for Its Own Sake

A FUNDAMENTAL ERROR, which has countless consequences, is the notion that change is the sign of life. I spoke of this in detail in my books *The Trojan Horse* and *Celibacy and the Crisis of Faith*. But this error, this infatuation with the dynamic and this denial of the high value of the static, is so widespread, so responsible for the manifold nonsense in the liturgy — in all external forms — that I cannot do otherwise than briefly to point it out in this book as well. Here is the root of much of the devastation of the vineyard of the Lord. This infatuation with change as such is as silly and infantile as its consequences are irreverent and evil.

The claim that change is the sign of life is a mere slogan. It is correct that in the sphere of life — as distinguished from the sphere of mere matter — a growing, a changing, and a development are present. But in all this development there is an identity which is given side by side with the changing: the individual plant, the individual animal. With-

78

out this identity it would no longer be a living creature. Indeed, it would not even be a real thing.

But if it is a matter of spiritual realities such as works of art, then it is an unconditional requirement that they remain unchanged. If, as unfortunately happens sometimes today, one were to perform an opera in an altered form, whether by changing the original scenery, or having the singers appear in modern clothing, or arbitrarily abridging it, this would only be admissible if the artistic value of the piece were thereby heightened. But in general these "changes" are made for the sake of change and novelty.

Plato says, "Every change is an evil, if it does not consist in the abolition of something negative."[35] The same goes for the changing of laws, classical forms of life, etc.

What concerns us here, however, is rather the infantile satisfaction which many people derive from change: the feeling of not being passive and inert. Now, the preservation of the good, and opposition to the rhythm of change, is a much greater achievement. To keep one's love for a person eternally youthful, above all to grow in one's love for Christ — which, however, also represents a stability, a holding fast — is a much greater sign of spiritual strength and life than becoming unfaithful.

Above all, we must not forget that the change present in growth, in which something new replaces something old, and the change which involves the destruction of something, are two completely different things.

But in our context what is above all decisive is whether we are dealing with growth in good, or in evil. The change which is contained in growth is a value when it is a change for the better, and a disvalue when for the worse.

Now there is also a growth in the sense of a transition from implicit to explicit — a growth toward detailed, clear formulation. This kind of growth is in opposition to change in the full sense. It is a movement which is radically opposed to the destruction of something and the substitution of something else in its place.

It is a movement in which identity, the absence of all change, is the conspicuous and decisive thing. That is the miracle of the Church throughout the 2000 years of her existence. Read Denzinger[36] and you will be overwhelmed by the growth in the elaboration of the true Revelation of Christ. It becomes more and more sealed off from all possible misinterpretations. And in this repudiation of all heresy, the authentic content of Christian Revelation becomes formulated in more and more detail, whereby we find a direct line of development from the earlier to the later formulations.

This absolute identity in the teaching of the Church, in which new dogmas are added to already existing ones, yet without eliminating them, or contradicting them in any way, is a magnificent proof of the divine institution of the Church as the guardian of the Revelation of Christ.

We have already spoken of the high value of stability, of not being changed, in *Celibacy and the Crisis of Faith*:

"It is an illusion deeply rooted in human nature that it is a sign of being awake and alive when one changes existing things. To leave things as they are is regarded as a sign of inertness and ossification, whereas one is thought to be doing something important in intervening and changing. This is particularly the illusion of those who occupy a certain office or official position. But this overlooks that the protection and preservation of good things is a great sign of being awake and alive and is often a far more difficult task than changing and intervening. But the decisive error — the illusion of

seeing in change as such a sign of being awake and alive —
comes from forgetting that the meaning and value of any
change or preservation depends exclusively upon the things
which are changed or preserved. If something is bad, then
it should be changed if possible. If something is good and
valuable, it is required of us that we strive to preserve it and
keep it in existence." [37]

Truth is essentially unchangeable. But man is very changeable. The stability of all great and good things is a high value.
Growth, in the sense of the increase of our love for God or
for a friend or one's wife or husband, is a heightening and a
deepening in which everything which was there before lives
on and does not disappear.

But what is important to us here is the value of stability
as opposed to change, [38] as far as it is a matter of something
good and beautiful. As soon as a disvalue comes into question, then change — indeed the complete elimination of the
disvalue — is a great value.

But let us now remain in the sphere of the good and the
beautiful. The structure of the whole liturgical year and the
Tridentine Mass was something great and wonderful. It was
of greatest pastoral importance as a way of drawing us up
from the whole mediocrity of everyday life, indeed from the
finite and worldly sphere into the world of supernatural
mystery, into the world of Christ.

Here the thought of a change and reform is meaningless.
This is not only because we live in a time in which the talent
for the formation of the liturgy is very weak, as we already
mentioned, but also because this work has been entrusted to
"experts," and not to men who are filled with great reverence
for that which has been handed down to us from earlier,
glorious times — indeed entrusted to men who base their

work on a false diagnosis of our time, on the myth of "modern man."

But what we want to emphasize here is the value of stability, the value which lies in praying in the same way in which the saints and *"homines religiosi"* of the past prayed. Here the great community unfolds of which we have already spoken, for it is related to the past as well as to the present.

A dilettante changing for the sake of change is not only an infantile procedure, but leads also to a disastrous confusion in its pedagogical effects.[39]

NOTES

35. *Laws,* no. 797.

36. Heinrich Denzinger, *Enchiridion Symbolorum,* 34th revised edition (New York: Herder, 1967). There is also this reason why Denzinger is a highly edifying book: it shows the role which dogmatic questions have played in Christianity.

37. *Celibacy and the Crisis of Faith* (Chicago: Franciscan Herald Press, 1971), xxxix.

38. The famous statement of Cardinal Newman is no contradiction of what we are saying: "In a higher world it is otherwise, but here below to live is to change, and to be perfect is to have changed often." This means that we often find ourselves in circumstances where a change is objectively called for and is thus a sign of life, not that a change for its own sake is a sign of life. Furthermore, Newman is here speaking of changes undertaken for the purpose of preserving; for, the preceding sentence is: "It (an idea in development) changes with them (its circumstances) in order to remain the same."

39. We have spoken in detail of the value of tradition in *The Trojan Horse in the City of God* (Chicago: Franciscan Herald Press, 1967), esp. Ch. 28.

10

The Idolization of Learning

> It is to get rid of doing God's will that we have in-
> vented learning . . . we shield ourselves by hiding behind
> tomes. — Kierkegaard[40]

NOW WE HAVE TO ANALYZE still another error which is widespread at the present time, one which is also responsible to
a large extent for the mutilation of the liturgy: the idol of
learning and knowledge.

This is expressed on the one hand by the notion that it is
undemocratic and discriminatory for a person not to be able
to go to high school, college, or a university. It is forgotten
that study only has a meaning when a corresponding talent
is present. When one considers how a farmer, an artisan, an
employee, or a laborer can be a much more intelligent and
fulfilled person than a weak, ungifted teacher, or even professor,[41] then the madness of this idolization of learning and
knowledge becomes evident. The greater the tension between
the immanent claim of an activity and its vocational fulfill-

ment, the more unfulfilled is the life of this man, and the more unfortunate it is for others, and the less is his work a source of happiness for him.

In this sense Mortimer Smith has written in his excellent book, *And Madly Teach,* "Thus arises competence without intelligence."

A further symptom of this idolization of learning is the fact that one has completely forgotten the difference between the things of which knowledge, however interesting it may be in itself, does not make a man richer, fuller, or happier, unless he has a special talent for them. If we ask ourselves honestly whether it enriches every man to know what an imaginary number is, or that there are cosmic rays, or certain facts of chemistry, then one cannot deny that it makes no great difference for his life, for his understanding of the world, for his personality, whether he knows it or not. If he has no special interest in these sciences, no clear talent for them, then this knowledge does not enrich his life.

But there are many things, whose knowledge really does mean an enrichment, an expansion of the horizons for every man. To these belong, for example, the knowledge of different languages, at least to the extent of being able to speak and read them. We are not thinking in the first place of the practical utility of the knowledge of different languages, but rather of the enrichment deriving from contact with the "world," the atmosphere of other nations as expressed through their languages.[42] The same is true of the knowledge of history. Here also the knowledge of great and important events of the past is an enriching factor for everyone.

What we have just been considering, however, is more the question of what contributes to true "education," i.e., what belongs to an educated man. This only concerns the question of what should receive more emphasis in general education, but does not concern our actual problem, which is the exaggerated cult of learning.

It cannot be denied that a simple, uneducated man can be much more interesting, personally rich, and intelligent than one who has studied a good deal. I am not here questioning the value of education itself; but to esteem it highly is in no way to succumb to the idol of learning. One makes an idol of learning when one maintains that the education which has been gained by study is the only form of learning in the broader sense, and even that it is the only way of enriching, fulfilling, and giving meaning to human life.

Up into the nineteenth century, the *pater familias* among Italian farmers, especially in Tuscany, often sang a *canto* from Dante's *Divina Commedia* to his family, although he could perhaps hardly read and write. This was certainly a striking sign of authentic education. Certainly he must have become acquainted with the *Divina Commedia* through his father, or someone else, but this obviously occurred in the form of tradition, not by study in school, and even less in university courses.

But a much worse consequence of the idol of learning is the killing of common sense, which is being undertaken on a widespread scale in grammar schools, high schools, and colleges.[43] One forgets the great source of wisdom which lies in our immediate contact with being, and how pernicious it is to replace the resulting world view, with instruction which draws its nourishment from doubtful psychological and sociological theories, and false, flat philosophies. Every immediate, true experience in which the voice of being speaks to a person, is much more interesting than the questionable theories he has adopted concerning the world and life.

Thus it is that a simple, unlettered man, when he speaks about the world and his life, is much wiser, much truer, and more genuine than all the half-educated people who simply repeat the stupid theories expounded by their professors.[44] The statement of a simple person may be clumsily expressed; it may be incomplete, and even contain errors. But it will always have a kernel of truth, always the freshness of a genuine contact with reality, and be free from the arrogant presumption of establishing a valid theory in the sense of looking "behind the scenes" of reality, and being able to "explain" everything. The dangerous error of the cult of teaching and learning reaches its climax in the ambition to improve, modify, or even replace natural, immediate, organic contact with the world and life, by an artificial contact based on so-called "scientific" theories.

A sad example of this is the nonsense of "enlightenment" in the schools with regard to sexual matters. It is believed that the laboratory attitude is the *causa exemplaris* (model) of a rational, healthy attitude towards all things and all questions. According to such a view, neutral "objectivization," the attitude of a detached observer is not only the only source of true knowledge — already a sufficiently catastrophic error — but also the desirable form of all immediate contact in life, and of the experiencing of everything.

The idol of teaching and learning bears within itself the seeds of destruction of all true education, of all true upbringing, of a humanly healthy, genuine life, and of all true happiness.

And now it is not difficult to see that the penetration of this idol into the Church bears part of the blame for the unfortunate mutilation of the liturgy and the destruction of the organic structure of the liturgical year.

One is coming more and more to believe that the important thing at Mass is knowledge, and that for true participation in the Sacrifice of the Mass the understanding of every word is more essential than recollection, than going into one's personal depths, than the reverent immersion of oneself in the mystery of the unbloody Sacrifice on the Cross. For true participation at Holy Mass, it is important for the faithful that the priest as an individual person become completely absorbed in his role of representing Christ, that everything else disappear except the incredible mystery of the unbloody renewal of the Sacrifice of the Cross. The dialogue of the priest in the holy Mass, the *Dominus vobiscum, Orate fratres,* and the dialogue before the Preface, are all one dialogue which is built into the sacred happening of the Mass; it is precisely a sacred dialogue and not an imparting of information about the kind of Preface and Canon being used. Today it is becoming more and more common for the priest to interrupt the service to speak to the faithful, to instruct them about the progress of the Mass. This should take place beforehand, in catechetical classes, or at most in the sermon, but never in the course of the sacred action, where the priest represents Christ, and the faithful are completely caught up in *participating* in the sacred event.[45]

This indicates a misunderstanding of the fact that there is an abyss between the attitude of being instructed and of studying on the one hand, and of participating in an event or happening, or expressing an inner attitude on the other hand. In the case of learning, of profane instruction, there is a "consciousness of" something, but in performing some act, although I am certainly directed to an object, and although there is also a transcending of myself as in the case of knowledge, nevertheless the response which I give interiorly is of a different nature, it is itself a conscious entity, a cooperation with the object. Adoration, and the inner participation in Christ's sacrifice on the Cross in holy Mass, must be inwardly lived out, and if the priest interrupts with comments about the Mass which are related to practical details, then the faithful are necessarily taken out of the attitude of participation and drawn into an attitude of being informed. Indeed, they are taken out of the sacred dialogue which is part of the holy Mass.

The difference between the attitude of participation, and of being informed in a neutral way, becomes clear if we draw a comparison from the natural sphere. If someone who deeply loves a woman declares his love for her for the first time, his declaration is not neutral information, but a declaration of his love; the words have a completely different function here than in a lecture or a textbook. They are, as it were, the medium through which the ray of his love penetrates into the soul of the beloved, really touching her. The theme is not a mere piece of information *about* a fact, but an affecting of the soul of the beloved. And if she receives the declaration of love in the way it is meant, it is no instruction, but a deeply moving and unique experience of being loved. Obviously this is separated by an abyss from merely finding out about a fact, from receiving mere neutral instruction or information. Therefore, it is completely meaningful — and even required — that this declaration of love be repeated over and over again.

But even the public reading of the Epistle and the Gospel in the first part of the holy Mass, the so-called "Mass of the Catechumens," is not "instruction" in the strict sense of the word. The reading should enlighten our mind and draw us into the sacral world of the mystery of the Mass. What happens and should happen here is not a neutral imparting of information about the holy Mass, as for example a comment by a deacon on what the priest is now doing, or a technical instruction about something concerning this particular Mass. Rather it is the word of God coming to us through a prophet or an apostle, a summons which should awaken us, drawing our soul into God's presence (*conspectus Dei*). This is true to a still greater extent, i.e., we reach yet a higher level, when the holy Gospel is read, when it is the words of the same Christ who after the consecration is bodily present and whom we receive into our souls in Holy Communion. It is the inconceivably Holy One, the God-Man Jesus Christ, who speaks to us: to each one of us individually, and to all of us together. No one can overlook the abyss which even on a purely formal level separates this proclamation of the words and deeds of Christ and our hearing of them, from a neutral instruction.

If a sermon is given on Sundays and holy days, then it should awaken the souls of the faithful so that they might be illumined by the incomprehensible glory of the Gospel. The sermon ought to show in detail the call of Christ and all the consequences of this call, as well as point out the dangers which hinder the growth of the true seed of Christ in the soul. We need only think of the sermons of St. Leo, St. Augustine, or Cardinal Newman in order to see clearly how the sermon organically fits into the preparatory part of holy Mass and how greatly it differs from a purely informative instruction.

NOTES

40. Kierkegaard, quoted in Lowrie, *Kierkegaard* (New York: Harper, 1962), Vol. II, p. 539.

41. One could object that this perhaps used to be true, but that in an industrialized world, in which so many workers must exercise a com-

pletely mechanical function every day for hours on end, one cannot deny that such work cannot enrich any man or be a source of happiness for him. That is certainly true, but it is only an objection to the industrialization of the world, but no justification for the idolization of learning. For it is doubtful whether academic studies are the only way to fill up the emptiness which has arisen through an over-mechanization in the life of man.

42. Latin is in a unique position here. First, Latin grammar has an uncommon clarity, and to know it, is an incomparable training for our thinking. Secondly, Latin has a great beauty, a spiritual nobility of quite a special sort. This is also true of medieval Latin, which moreover produced works of highest poetical art and religious depth. One need only think of the *Dies irae,* which is ascribed to Thomas of Celano, of Jacapone da Todi's *Stabat mater,* of the magnificent hymns of St. Thomas Aquinas, of the sequences of Venantius Fortunatus, and many others. The role which Latin has played in history, especially in the liturgy, and the universality which it possesses, gives the learning of Latin quite a special place.

43. Cf. Marcel de Corte, *L'Intelligence en Péril de Mort* (Paris: Collection du Club de la Culture Française, 1969).

44. "Your modern educator is anti-intellectual and anti-cultural, practical and narrowly scientific." Mortimer Smith, *And Madly Teach.*

45. All explanations by the celebrant during the Preface and Canon have been forbidden by the *Instructio* of the Sacred Congregation for Divine Worship, issued on April 27, 1973, and approved by Pope Paul.

11
"Ecumenitis"

IN MY *Trojan Horse* I spoke of the true meaning of ecumenism and of the many dangerous misinterpretations of it in the
post-conciliar period. The justified demand that we do not
view schismatics, Protestants, Jews, Moslems, Brahmans, and
Buddhists solely as enemies, that we not only emphasize their
errors, but also recognize the positive elements of their religion: this was the original intent of ecumenism. That our relation to schismatics is different from our relation to Protestants
was already emphasized in the first encyclical of Paul VI,
Ecclesiam suam. The former are only schismatics; the Protestants, on the other hand, are separated from us by matters of
dogma. Still more different is our relation with all non-Christians. Here again it makes a great difference whether we are
dealing with monotheists, such as Jews and Moslems, or with
religions which are not monotheistic. But in all ecumenism
this remains required of us: even for the sake of unity we

must make no compromises whatever which would sacrifice even one iota of the *depositum catholicae fidei.*

Here we are especially interested in our relation to the Jews. With them we have a particular bond, insofar as they also acknowledge the Old Testament as authentic Revelation of God. On the other hand there is a unique opposition because they deny the Revelation of God in Christ and regard it as a specific distortion.

Now strangely enough, misunderstood ecumenism, a disease which one could call ecumenitis, has led to surprising results. There is a widespread tendency in the Church today to view the religion of Israel as a parallel way to God, one which is perhaps only less complete than the Christian way. We are told that one should no longer seek to convert the Jews; one should, with respect and esteem, let them go their own way.

This conception is obviously in radical contradiction to the words of Christ and the intention of the Apostles. Did Christ not in many places give expression to His sorrow that the Jews did not recognize Him? Were not the Apostles and disciples Jews to whom He had proclaimed the Divine Revelation? When Christ asked the disciples, "Who do you say that I am," did not Peter say to Him, "Thou art the Christ, the Son of the Living God" (Mt. 16:16)? And was not the first task of the Apostles after Pentecost the conversion of the Jews to the full Christian Revelation? When the Jews asked the Apostles, "Brothers, what should we do?" Peter replied, "Repent and be baptized" (Acts 2:37). Did not St. Paul speak of the conversion of the Jews as the great goal, and say, "For the sake of their disbelief, they were uprooted" (Rom. 11:20), and further, "But even they will be established again if they do not harden in their disbelief"

(Rom. 11:23)? Is it not the evident conviction of all Catholics and Protestants that the New Testament is the fulfillment of the Old Testament? This relation of Christianity to the Mosaic religion is incomparably deeper than the fact that both recognize the Old Testament as Divine Revelation.

Apart from this contradiction with the words of Christ and the Apostles, indeed with the whole teaching of the Church, this notion of leaving the Jews alone shows a very great lack of love for the Jews. For the deepest core of true love of neighbor is the concern for the eternal salvation of the neighbor. Therefore, one should encounter no man without seeing in him a living member of the Mystical Body of Christ or a catechumen *in spe* (a prospective catechumen).

Let it not be objected that he can also attain his eternal salvation outside the Church, as a Protestant or as a non-Christian. This is, of course, a dogma which was defined at the First Vatican Council, but it changes nothing of the mission which Christ gave us: "Go forth into all the world and teach all peoples and baptize them," nor of the enormous importance of the adoration of God in truth, in Christ, *per ipsum, cum ipso, et in ipso.* There is after all an infinite value in the glorification of God which is present in the true Faith, in union with God through sanctifying grace and all the sacraments. And this desire to glorify God in an apostolate which flows from the true love of Christ, cannot be separated from true love of neighbor, which is grounded in the love of Christ alone.

A polite respect for the Jews takes the place of true love — a typical case of "this-worldliness" (which we will examine in detail in the second part of this book).

But it is still worse that the Old Testament is no longer seen as ordered to the New. Is Christ *the* Messiah, of whom

Isaias speaks? Is He the Son of God who redeemed mankind? If so, then the expectation of another Messiah is a clear error and not a parallel way to God. In the light of truth and before God this claim is a betrayal of Christ and a denial of the fact that the Revelation of the Old Testament is an essential part of Christian Revelation.

Is Christ the Son of God — the God of Abraham, Isaac, and Jacob? Is He the Redeemer, promised by God to Abraham? Did Christ not say, "Abraham saw my day and rejoiced" (John 8: 56)? And did He not also say, "I am not come to abolish the Law, but to fulfill it" (Mt. 5: 17)? How is it possible that ecumenitis has brought fruits which are in radical contradiction to the Gospel, to the Apostles, and to the teaching of the Church?

If the attitude of some in positions of authority toward the conversion of the Jews is in flagrant contradiction to the whole Gospel and to the Epistles of St. Paul, the widespread attitude towards the reception of non-Catholics into the holy Church is in just as radical an opposition to the Gospel. There are many theologians, pastors, and even missionaries today who propagate the viewpoint that the conversion of individual men to the Catholic Church is not the real work of the Church, they say that the Church should aim at uniting with entire religious communities, yet without requiring them to change their belief. This is supposed to be the goal of true ecumenism. To the individual Protestant, Moslem, or Hindu, who in the true sense of the word wants to convert, one should rather say that he should become a better Protestant, a better Moslem, a better Hindu. Have these theologians, priests, and missionaries never read the Gospel? Or have they forgotten that before His Ascension Christ said, "Go forth into all the world, and announce the Good News to all creatures. He who believes and is baptized will be saved, but he who does not believe will be condemned" (Mark 16:15-16)?

This monstrosity of ecumenitis combines many serious errors: it is, in the first place, an express ignoring of the mandate of Christ. In the second place, it shows a terrible disregard for the value of God's revelation for non-Christians: it means acting as though God's revelation in Christ and the death of Christ on the cross were superfluous for them. For from the standpoint of this ecumenitis, all men, especially Jews, would have been saved anyway, as long as they had lived in accordance with their respective beliefs. In the third place, there is here an absolute lack of interest in the truth. The question of which is the true religion no longer plays a role. The ultimate seriousness of truth, on which every religion stands or falls, is ignored. The essence, and the justification for the existence of the holy Church, is thereby destroyed, as indeed is the entire Christian religion. The teaching of the Church is either the true Revelation of God, the Revelation of Christ and absolutely and unconditionally true — or it is nothing. With this is connected, in the fourth place, the elimination of the glorification of God; only the salvation of men still plays a role. We have pointed out already that the glorification of God demands that He is adored in truth, and that this glorification does not occur when He in His infinite mercy grants eternal beatitude to a man who is not a member of the Mystical Body of Christ. In a similar fashion, the glorification of God through the saints is overlooked. For there can only be saints in the holy Church, in absolute imitation of Christ.

Finally, in the fifth place, the highpoint of depersonalization, of collectivism is manifested in the fact that the individual person no longer plays a role, but only the community.

The individual need not convert, need not be led from darkness into light; he need not fully experience and know the Revelation of Christ; he need not participate in the supernatural life of grace through baptism and in the stream of grace in the other sacraments. It is desirable only that all the religious communities be externally joined together.

But this would never effect a unity; it would remain a pure addition. Such an endeavor is the typical monstrous product of the grave error of placing unity above truth. We will discuss this later. Is it not clear that this external union would in no sense be a glorification of God and in no way a fulfillment of the solemn mandate of Christ, nor of His prayer, "That all may be one"?

The apostolate belongs essentially to the holy Church — the apostolate and indeed the conversion of every individual soul, which is more important in the eyes of the Church than the fate of any natural community. This flows necessarily from the love of God as well as from the true love of neighbor. The love of God impels the Church, but also every true Christian, to bring each man into the full light of truth, which is the teaching of the holy Church. Every Christian must long for all men to become acquainted with the Revelation of Christ and to respond to it with faith, for every knee to bend to Jesus Christ. And similarly true love of neighbor requires this. How can I love somebody and not ardently desire that he become acquainted with Jesus Christ, the begotten Son and Epiphany of God, that he be drawn into His light, believe in Him and love Him, and know that he is loved by Him? How can I love him without desiring for him even on earth the blissful encounter with Jesus Christ, which is the greatest source of happiness? How can I content myself with the fact that God's infinite mercy will — perhaps — not refuse him eternal beatitude in spite of his erroneous beliefs, or lack of faith? Truly, all deeds of love for my neighbor are only the noise of "sounding brass" if I am uninterested in his finding the true God, and in his becoming a member in the Mystical Body of Christ: if I am uninterested in his greatest good.

We see that ecumenitis can lead to the most horrible errors, and unfortunately it already has in many respects. This has nothing to do with the spirit of true ecumenism, and indeed stands in radical contradiction to it.

12

Is Schism the Greatest Evil?

IN VARIOUS PLACES we have pointed out the reasons why the *anathema* has been brought into disrepute: false irenicism, reluctance to make full use of authority, human respect, placing unity over truth.

But one factor which also plays a large role in all this is the fear of schism. The condemnation of a prominent heretic can naturally lead to a schism. His adherents, as well as many who view the *anathema* as medieval fanaticism, can make such a condemnation the occasion for falling away from the Church and becoming an independent sect.

But is a schism truly the greatest evil? The falling away of each individual person who leaves the Church is a great evil in itself, and especially for his soul, endangering his eternal salvation. But it is much worse when, although he has lost the true faith, he remains within the Church and poisons the faithful through his influence. This is worse for him too, because he adds to the awful sin of heresy that of lying, deceiving others, abusing his dignity as a Catholic, and, in the case of a priest, abusing the trust which he possesses as a spokesman for the Church. But schism is more than the falling away of a single Catholic. It is the separation of a part of the Church from Rome, the refusal to recognize the pope as the head of the Church, the establishment of a separate, independent church.

Schism can also be coupled with an apostasy from the teaching of the Church — as, with heresies — but it need not be. There may be a separation which is not brought about by dogmatic differences. This is the case, for example, with the Orthodox Church. Only in the eleventh century did it come to a definitive separation, that is, the severance of the Eastern Church. Certainly there had also been theological differences before this. But the dogmatic distinction of *"filioque"* was more an excuse for the schism, which came about essentially for political reasons. This schism was a great evil, and the destruction of unity was a great catastrophe, which from a dogmatic standpoint was unnecessary. It was a pure evil.

In the case of the schism of the Reformation, on the other hand, the dogmatic differences were decisive. This was an apostasy from the *depositum catholicae fidei*: heresy, the greatest evil. Thus this schism, this destruction of unity, was an unavoidable, indeed necessary consequence of the heresy. In this case, it was better that a schism occur than that the heretics remain within the Church and endanger the true belief of all the faithful. It was to the great merit of the Council of Trent that it clearly emphasized the heresy of the Protestants, and that it saved the holy Church from inner disintegration. The great tragedy here lay in the heresy, and not in the schism which was connected with it. In this case it would have been incomparably worse if, for the sake of maintaining unity, one had compromised with the Protestants, if one had blurred the dogmatic division, and had thus permitted a destructive poison to remain within the organism of the Church.

Unity is of great value, but only unity in truth. This is also the only true unity. Fidelity to Divine Revelation, which is fidelity towards God, is infinitely more important than all unity.

Another view often comes up in the discussion of schism, however, which has a meaning in relation to a natural community, but which is completely irrelevant to the supernatural community of the Church. In many natural communities size plays a decisive role. The effectiveness of a political party in achieving its goal is dependent upon its size. The number of members therefore has a decisive importance for the party (but not for the individual). Its size is decisive for its power, and in this case the question of power is a highly significant factor.

But in the case of the Church the question of power in this sense becomes irrelevant. Her goal is that all men find the way to truth and to eternal beatitude. Membership in the Catholic Church is an absolute value for every individual soul, indeed the highest good on earth. When I say membership, I mean thereby integral faith in the Revelation of Christ, as it is laid down in the *depositum catholicae fidei,* the love for Christ, obedience to the commandments of the Church: in short, not merely the baptismal certificate. To this is added a second high value: the spreading of the Kingdom of God. The conversion of every individual is not only primarily a glorification of God and secondarily the highest good for his soul, but it is also a glorification of God through the growth of the Mystical Body of Christ.

It is a greater evil for a heretic to remain in the Church, however, than for the Church to become poorer by one member. It is better that he leave the Church, or be excluded from her by *anathema* or by excommunication. This is not only better from the standpoint of the Church and all the faithful, but also for the soul of the heretic, because he becomes more conscious of his apostasy from the true Faith, and can thereby possibly be brought to his senses.

The view that a natural community is weakened — indeed declines and even disintegrates — when it loses members has unfortunately crept unconsciously even into our judgment of the evil of schism, causing many compromises to be made at the expense of orthodoxy for no better reason than to avoid a decrease in size.

Are not these words of Christ true analogously for the excommunication of a heretic:

"But if thy hand or thy foot scandalize thee, cut it off and throw it away! It is better for thee to enter into life crippled or lamed than to be cast into the eternal fire with two hands or feet. And if thine eye scandalize thee, tear it out and throw it away. It is better for thee to enter into life with one eye than to be cast into hell with two eyes" (Mt. 18:8-10).

13
Dawn

IF WE COMPARE the Church's present situation with the situation in 1967, the year in which I wrote *The Trojan Horse,* we will discover that, as we said at the beginning of this book, the comparison with the Trojan Horse is no longer apt. We must now speak of a devastation of the vineyard of the Lord, which is still advancing daily. But the situation has also changed inasmuch as the opposition to this devastation has greatly increased, and many voices are being raised in defense of orthodoxy. Indeed, we see an unmistakeable wave of awakening, of protest against heresies.

In many countries orthodox Catholics have formed associations which are courageously taking up the battle against the grave-diggers of the Church. Many of these Catholics, writing in various magazines, come to the defense of the undistorted faith, untarnished by compromises of any kind; they defend the primacy of the glorification of God through the sanctification of the individual soul, the conversion of all men to Christ, and salvation of souls. These people understand the magnificence of the holy Church, and her glorious past as proclaimer of the Revelation of God throughout 2000 years, as the fortress against all heresies, as the Mother of countless saints, and they are filled with a true love for her. Though there may be individual differences among these Catholics, they all are fighting the devastation of the vineyard of the Lord.

Furthermore, certain theologians who were at first infected by progressivism have in the meantime recognized the danger of the situation in the holy Church, and have returned to orthodoxy. And above all, we sometimes encounter saintly persons who have remained utterly unharmed in their faith by the devastation of the Church.

This is all a great consolation, and it is especially a hope for the future. This is real progress, progress in the ranks of the faithful who are fighting the devastation of the vineyard of the Lord which is raging under the influence of Teilhardism and such slogans as *aggiornamento,* and "adaptation to the spirit of the age." In the Third Roman Synod in September and October, 1971, we already saw a conscious and successful opposition to the destructive tendencies of the modern "reformers." Responding to the unambiguous position of the Holy Father, the majority of the College of Bishops followed the lead of Cardinals Bengsch and Hoeffner.

Another encouraging sign is the fact that Cardinal Suenens was sharply criticized in *Osservatore Romano,* and that Cardinal Daniélou publicly challenged him in *Figaro.*[46] This is an indication that one no longer refrains from unmasking even cardinals who are participating in the devastation of the vineyard.

The decree concerning the dress of religious (especially

of nuns, which we have mentioned already) places limits on experiments.

But the General Catechetical Directory is a special indication that the hierarchy is becoming more and more conscious of the dangers and trying to fight them. Another very special sign of this is the letter from Cardinal Garrone to all seminaries regarding the role of philosophy and the disastrous effect of false philosophies on the seminarians and future priests. I quote from the letter sent in January:

"There can be no doubt that modern culture, in closing its eyes more and more to the problem of transcendence, is becoming adverse to authentic philosophical thought, especially to metaphysics, which alone is able to reach absolute values. In this regard, first of all, one must mention the modern spirit of technology, which has a tendency to make a mere *homo faber* out of *homo sapiens*. . . . The unilateral emphasis which is laid on action directed to the future, and the optimism which is nourished by an almost boundless confidence in progress, which aimed at immediate and fundamental changes in the economic, social, and political realms, tend to overlook the unchangeable character of certain moral and spiritual values. Above all, authentic philosophical speculation, which has to be taught as the indispensable basis for these changes, is held to be superfluous, or even detrimental. In such a climate the serious investigation of the highest truths is not appreciated, and the criteria of truth are no longer the solid, indubitable principles of metaphysics, but rather the 'present epoch' and 'success.' Therefore it is easy to understand how the spirit of our time shows itself to be increasingly anti-metaphysical and thus open to all forms of relativism. . . . When one keeps all this in mind, one can ascertain in general that the true essence of the Judaeo-Christian Revelation is absolutely incompatible with all epistemological, ethical, and metaphysical relativism, as well as with all materialism, pantheism, immanentism, subjectivism, and atheism."[47]

In March of 1972 the Sacred Congregation for the Doctrine of the Faith, whose Prefect is Cardinal Seper, issued a document which was ratified, confirmed, and designated for publication by the Holy Father, and which was directed in a special way against certain errors which are endangering faith in the mysteries of the Incarnation and of the Holy Trinity. It is to be hoped that this document will have further consequences.

And then on June 24, 1973, the same Congregation issued an important document (from which we quoted above) entitled, "Declaration in Defense of the Catholic Doctrine on the Church, against Certain Errors of the Day." In this document it is first of all reaffirmed that the Roman Catholic Church is identical with the Church of Christ. Then the errors of Küng on infallibility are directly condemned, as are those errors (also held by Küng) which say that new dogmatic formulations have to be found for the Revelation of Christ, or that no possible dogmatic formulations are strictly true.

But the most important thing is the intervention of the Holy Father in Holland when he appointed two orthodox bishops.

I would like to conclude these signs of hope with the words of the Holy Father in the audience already cited, on January 19, 1972,[48] in which he himself takes a position toward burning problems:

"So it is, beloved sons. And in affirming this, we repudiate those errors which were already in circulation formerly, which are running rampant again in the spiritual life of our time, and which could completely destroy our Christian understanding of life and history. Modernism was the characteristic expression of these false doctrines; it is, under other names, still influential today (cf. the decree *Lamentabili* of Pius X, 1907, and his encyclical *Pascendi;* Denz.-Sch., 3401 ff). We can now understand why the Catholic Church, now as in the past, attributes such importance to the strict preservation of the authentic Revelation, and views it as an inviolable treasure, and why she has such a strict notion of her fundamental duty to defend the doctrines of the Faith, and to transmit them in an unequivocal form. Orthodoxy is her main concern, and the pastoral office is her most important, divinely willed mission. The teaching of the Apostles in fact determines the canon of her proclamation. The instruction of the Apostle Paul, "Preserve what has been entrusted to you!" (1 Tim. 6:20; 2 Tim. 1:14) presents her with a duty which it would be betrayal not to observe. The Church as teacher does not invent her doctrine; she gives testimony, preserves, presents, mediates. If it is a matter of the truth of the message of the Gospel, the Church can be characterized as conservative and implacable. To those who would like to induce the Church to simplify her Faith and conform to the taste of the changeable spirit of the age, she replies with the Apostles, '*Non possumus!*' 'We cannot!' " (Acts 4:20).

NOTES

46. Cardinal Daniélou clearly condemned "progressivism" in an important speech in Washington in 1970. Cf. *Celibacy and the Crisis of Faith,* p. 138.

47. From the letter of the Sacred Congregation for Catholic Education, "To the Ordinaries of the World on the Study of Philosophy in Seminaries," Prot. N. 137/65, dated Jan. 20, 1972; I, III, 2.

48. Quoted from *Osservatore Romano,* English edition, Jan. 26, 1972.

PART II

14

The Sacred Humanity of Jesus

$$\scriptstyle \texttt{:::}$$

> It is the manifestation of the glory of God in the Face
> of Jesus; it is that view of the attributes and perfec-
> tions of Almighty God; it is the beauty of His sanctity,
> the sweetness of His mercy, the brightness of His
> heaven, the majesty of His law, the harmony of His
> providences, the thrilling music of His voice, which is
> the antagonist of the flesh, and the soul's champion
> against the world and the devil. — Cardinal Newman[49]

WE NOW TURN TO the kind of devastation of the vineyard
of the Lord which does not express itself by open attacks
against the *depositum catholicae fidei,* by explicit, formal
heresies, but rather by tendencies which, like a creeping
poison, work in a still more dangerous way. Of course, these
tendencies always contain grave theological and philosophical
errors, but unlike explicit theses, they carry out their work
of destruction in an "underground" way, unfortunately usually without being recognized.

The most fundamental and catastrophic of these tendencies is the distortion of the sacred humanity of Christ, indeed
a false interpretation of the Incarnation.

It is overlooked that though Jesus ontologically possessed a fully human nature, he was qualitatively not an "average man," nor a man afflicted with all kinds of negative qualities, but the Holy One *par excellence*. At the beginning of St. John's Gospel we read, *"Et verbum caro factum est et habitavit in nobis et vidimus gloriam ejus gloriam quasi Unigeniti a Patre, plenum gratiae et veritatis"* ("And the Word was made Flesh and dwelt among us, and we have seen His glory, the glory of the only begotten Son of the Father, full of grace and truth."). These words not only testify to the incomprehensible, impenetrable mystery that the second divine person of the Blessed Trinity — the Logos — assumed a human nature, but also to the fact that this human nature is "full of grace and truth."

But by assuming human nature, the Logos in no sense loses His divine nature. Christ has two natures, a divine one and a human one. Although the two natures remain completely distinct ontologically, and are not mixed, yet in a mysterious way they are uniquely united, because they belong to one and the same Person. His sacred humanity is thus an *epiphany* of God. It is qualitatively formed by the holiness of God. *"Quia per incarnati Verbi mysterium nova mentis nostrae oculis lux Tuae claritatis infulsit — ut dum visibiliter Deum cognoscimus per hunc in invisibilium amorem rapiamur."* ("Because through the mystery of the Word made flesh the light of your glory has shone afresh upon the eyes of our mind, so that while we acknowledge Him to be God seen by men, we may be drawn by Him to the love of things unseen.") [50]

What concerns us here, however, is this: the fact that Christ was ontologically *totus homo* (fully man) in no way contradicts the fact that His sacred humanity is qualitatively an epiphany of God. When St. Paul saws he was like us in all things except sin, this must be understood to mean that He ontologically possessed all the susceptibilities and weaknesses of human nature, but no negative qualities at all. Thus He was not only free from sin in the strict sense, but also from all such negative things as mediocrity, narrowness, pettiness.

And here begins the horrible distortion of the humanity of Christ which we see today. It is explained that His human nature would only be fully human if it possessed qualitatively everything which we encounter in men — everything which characterizes the "average man." Certain modern catechisms emphasize how much Jesus liked a good meal. Books are being written about the sex life of Jesus, for this is supposed to belong to full humanity. After all, it is part of the Incarnation of God, so they say, that Jesus was fully man, *totus homo,* and that His human nature must therefore contain everything which occurs in man.

At this point, we must reflect on the essence of man, on that which distinguishes him ontologically from all other living creatures. For only then can the true meaning of *totus homo* be seen in its clear outlines.[51] Man alone is a conscious being, and this conscious being contains a completely new dimension of being. Scholastic philosophy very aptly named this kind of being "a being which possesses itself." Truly, an abyss separates material bodies such as rocks, or living matter such as a tree, or even living creatures such as animals, from man, who alone possesses the capacity for knowledge, free will, and responsibility. Man alone can be the bearer of moral values and disvalues. He alone is a person, and the difference between personal and apersonal is the greatest, most decisive metaphysical distinction of all, except for that between infinite and finite, between the absolute, eternal Person and the contingent person.

Man as a person is the only "awakened" being: all other forms which we find in nature are "asleep" so to speak. They only "undergo" being. Only man as a person can seek the truth, recognize and know truths; and above all: of man alone can St. Augustine say, *"Fecisti nos ad Te, Domine"* ("Thou hast made us for Thyself, O Lord."). Man alone can know the existence of God by his reason.

St. Bonaventure calls all the creatures on earth (pure matter, plants and animals) *"vestigia Dei,"* ("traces of God"). But because man is a person, he is the *imago Dei,* the "image of God." We are told in Genesis: "And God created man in His image." Human nature is ontologically characterized by being the image of God, inasmuch as it is a conscious being, a person.

But the ontological structure of man is not characterized solely by his being a person. Man, in contradistinction to God, the absolute Person, is a creaturely, contingent person. He is created, and only at the moment of conception does he begin to exist. He has not existed from all eternity. He is mortal, even though his soul is immortal. Though the angels are also created, contingent persons, they are pure spirits. Man on the other hand, is a creature consisting of a body and a soul. Human nature is characterized by this possession of body and soul and by the mysterious, deeply intimate union of body and soul, in spite of their clear and radical difference. We cannot go into all this in detail here; we can only point to some characteristics of human nature, the greatness and weakness of which were so magnificently portrayed by Pascal.[52] The soul is a conscious being and thus essentially, radically different from all matter: from lifeless matter as well as from living matter such as plants and animals. It differs above all from all physiological processes, including the chemical processes in the human brain. In my book, *The Sacred Heart,* I discussed in detail the various levels within the spiritual sphere, ranging from bodily pain up to the highest spiritual responses. Although in that work I limited myself to the affective sphere, the following things belong ontologically to human nature: a close union with the body, the weakness and susceptibility of man which results from it, as well as the capacity for suffering (from bodily pain up to spiritual pain), the ability to feel fear and anxiety, the metaphysical dependence on God, and much more.

When we speak of human nature from an ontological point of view, therefore, we mean the body-soul structure, and man's status as a person.

Before we analyze in detail the distinction which is decisive for us in our present context, the distinction between the qualitative and the ontological aspects of human nature, we still have to emphasize that Christ fully possessed a human nature ontologically, but that His *person* is not created, and is not a mere *imago Dei,* but rather the second Divine Person of the Blessed Trinity, who assumed a human nature. Therefore even from an ontological point of view there is an essential difference between Christ and all other men. We possess this truth by faith. But the Man Jesus in His inconceivable holiness was not only seen by the Apostles: we too encounter Him in the Gospels ontologically as a Man.

From an ontological point of view, Socrates had a human nature in common with Hitler and Stalin; they were created by God in His image. From an ontological point of view, they are the same kind of creature, namely human persons. But Socrates is obviously separated by an abyss from Hitler and

Stalin. This abyss is not related to the ontological structure of being human, but rather to the qualitative difference which exists between them: Socrates is a deeply moral man, an uncommonly noble personality, whereas Hitler was a criminal. Socrates was a great, an extraordinary thinker, whereas Hitler was a very confused, mediocre man.

We must now understand that the expression in the Creed *"totus homo"* refers to the ontological structure of man.

But we must also not forget the fundamental ontological difference between Jesus and all other men. This is due to the fact that although He possessed a human nature, His *person* was divine. He possessed a human and a divine nature in one person, but this person is the second Person of the Blessed Trinity: He is divine. This is certainly an impenetrable mystery, but it has been unequivocally revealed. In the Nicene or Chalcedonian Creed we say: *"Et in unum Dominum Jesum Christum, Filium Dei unigenitum. Et ex Patre Natum ante omnia saecula. Deum de Deo . . . Qui propter nos homines et propter nostram salutem descendit de caelis. Et incarnatus est de Spiritu Sancto ex Maria Virgine."* ("And in one Lord Jesus Christ, the only-begotten Son of God. Born of the Father before all ages. God of God . . . Who for us men and for our salvation came down from heaven. And was made flesh by the Holy Spirit of the Virgin Mary.") We find the same thing in the beginning of the Gospel according to St. John (John 1: 1-14), *"In principio erat Verbum, et Verbum erat apud Deum, et Deus erat Verbum. . . . et Verbum caro factum est."* ("In the beginning was the Word, and the Word was with God, and the Word was God . . . and the Word was made flesh.") All this shows clearly that it was the second Divine Person who assumed a human nature.

The *"totus homo"* refers to the ontological structure of

human nature, but in no way denies that the person is divine. Let us repeat: not only are a divine and a human nature united in one person in Jesus Christ, but this one person is self-identical with the second Person of the Blessed Trinity, the Logos. The Person of Jesus is not created; only the soul (and the body) of Jesus are created. The divine nature is inseparably united with the Person of Jesus, whereas the human nature is assumed by the Divine Person, even though as something which will continue to exist forever.

Our main concern here is with the qualitative distortion of the holy humanity of Jesus, and with the qualitative difference between Him and all other men. But this deep ontological difference must also be emphasized, impenetrable mystery as it is, for it in no way contradicts the *"totus homo."*

Terrible consequences follow from confusing the ontological structure of man with the qualitative nature, which varies so greatly among men.

Our ontological structure as man is that which unites us with all the saints, be it St. Francis of Assisi or St. John Bosco. Jesus shares this with us as well. But the qualitative abyss which separates us from these saints cannot be compared with that which separates us from the sacred humanity of Jesus, the epitome of all sanctity, who is only faintly reflected by all the saints. We are only referring to the sacred humanity of Jesus, of course, and not to the fact mentioned above, that we are confronted here with a Person who besides His human nature also possesses a divine nature, and whose person is divine. The divine nature of Christ is ontologically of course beyond any possible comparison — it is the ontological difference between the absolute Person of the Creator and the mere *imago Dei* of the creature.

Behind the distortion of the sacred humanity of Christ is

also a false concept of amplitude or breadth. One tries to smuggle in a denial of the incomprehensible holiness of the humanity of Jesus under the title "full man," and to render the personality of Jesus mediocre. There is hidden in the title "full man" not only the confusion between ontological and qualitative, but also the confusion between real amplititude, and a merely horizontal extension. Whereas one often used to make the mistake of thinking that we attain greater amplitude and breadth the more all-encompassing our concepts are, and thus of confusing the degrees of abstraction with the hierarchy of values, the present error is the incomparably more primitive, flat equation between the essence of man and the sum total of men. It is forgotten that to be a full man does not mean that one must himself potentially have all the qualitative characteristics which can be inherent in men. The "full" refers to the true essence of man, not to the sum total of men.

Jesus, according to His human nature — not His person — was an *imago Dei* ontologically, but qualitatively He possessed in His humanity not only the *similitudo Dei* — which it is our highest calling to attain, and which the saints did attain — but His humanity was an epiphany of God. It radiated the inconceivable holiness of God: "Philip, anyone who has seen me has seen the Father" (John 14: 9).

We must never forget that the "uninventable" humanity of Christ in its inconceivable holiness is the center of the Christian Revelation, and that it — more than all the miracles — is the greatest proof of the divinity of Christ. What compelled the Apostles — *"relictis omnibus"* ("leaving all things behind") — to follow the command *"sequere me"* ("follow me") and to fall down before Christ, was the epiphany of God in His holy humanity. The qualitative epiphany of God, the inconceivable holiness of Jesus is the basis for our belief in the impenetrable mystery of the Incarnation, in the fact that Christ is God, that the second Person of the Blessed Trinity assumed a human nature, without losing His divine nature.

The worst undermining of the Christian Faith, of the belief in the authentic Christian Revelation, of the teaching of the holy Church, is the distortion of the sacred humanity of Christ, the qualitative desacralization of the personality of Jesus.[53] All the pompous talk about the consequences of the Councils of Nicaea and Chalcedon supposedly having led to a one-sided emphasis on the divinity of Christ and to a neglect of the humanity of Christ, is a subtle and cunning attempt, in the guise of a seemingly historical, scientific, objective attitude, to open the door for the desacralization of the humanity of Jesus, for blinding us to the center of Revelation: the holy humanity of Jesus. In reality, the ontologically full humanity of Jesus, which lies in the expression *"totus Deus— totus homo"* ("fully God and fully man"), has always remained fully living in the holy Church. Think of the Franciscan movement, which introduced the special devotions to the Child Jesus and to the suffering of Jesus, in both of which the complete human nature of Christ becomes vivid. Think of the *"Stabat Mater dolorosa"* by Jacopone da Todi, of all the individualization in the representation of Christ in the art of the fourteenth and fifteenth centuries. But thank God the qualitative epiphany of God in Jesus' holy humanity was always seen and emphasized; one was fully Christian, and remained so.

Hand in hand with the profanation and desacralization of the holy humanity of Jesus goes logically the attempt to "reinterpret" all the miracles of Christ. This is cunningly done in the *Dutch Catechism for Adults*. For instance, the miracle of the Virgin Birth is denied in a cautious manner by speaking with sublime words of the creation of every human soul by God, then by speaking of the birth of Isaac and of St. John the Baptist as a heightening of the marvel which lies in every human birth, and finally by mentioning the birth of Jesus as the most marvelous birth of all. Thus in a seemingly reverent manner they explain away the fact that Jesus is not the son of Joseph, but the Son of God. The *"incarnatus est de spiritu sancto ex Maria virgine"* of the Creed is demythologized in Bultmann's sense. The same thing is done to the fundamental dogma of the Resurrection of Christ.

The attempt to make Christ mediocre, which is found in modern school catechisms, especially in some of the American ones, goes of course much further than the desacralization of the sacred humanity of Christ. Here not only is the holiness of Christ's human nature explained away on the grounds that Jesus is "fully human," not only is the epiphany of God in His holy humanity covered over, but the personality of Jesus is also made into a mediocre, average person. Holiness becomes a harmless geniality; the sublime spirit of Christ becomes average common sense. In short, the children are presented a personality which even in the sphere of human nature stands far beneath all the great and important historical figures. Under the guise of bringing Jesus nearer to the children, they distort the deeds and words of Christ in the Gospel, partly by leaving out the most important ones, partly by adding characteristics of Jesus which completely misrepresent His personality and which are completely arbitrary, without any basis in the Gospels. Thus Jesus becomes a harmless, average man, who is not worthy even to be the water-boy for Socrates or for the Gracchi, or for any genius.

Thank God the presentation of a "mediocre Jesus" is not yet as widespread as the desacralization of the sacred humanity of Christ. It cannot yet be found in the well-known theologians; it is not yet as widespread a tendency as is the desacralization of the sacred humanity of Jesus, which is even to be found in pastoral letters and sermons. But it is particularly disastrous from a pastoral viewpoint because it is presented to children in catechisms. Thus from the very beginning they receive a picture of Christ which renders faith in the divinity of Christ impossible. Only an idiotic child could believe that this "jolly good fellow" is the Son of God!

The desacralization of the holy humanity of Jesus and above all the presentation of a "mediocre Jesus" is incomparably more dangerous than the open denial of the divinity of Christ, which is often repeated by free-thinkers. I am not thinking of Arianism in this connection, which was an invasion of Plotinism into the holy Church. For the Arians Christ still remained the *Logos*: the ontologically highest being after God (*homoiusios* instead of *homousios* (like God instead of equal to God). He still had a relation to God which was completely different from that of a mere man. No, we are thinking of the denial of the divinity of Christ by the liberal Protestant theologians, of the claim that Christ was only a particularly noble man, but not the Son of God. Here the divine nature of Christ is simply denied. The Person of Christ here is no longer identical with the second Person of the Trinity, nor does He possess a divine nature. Christ is just a man like all the others, even though He is the most perfect man. These liberal theologians often no longer believe in the Trinity, and sometimes not even in the existence of God.

This attack on the divinity of Christ, which denies all ontological union with God, is less dangerous, or let us say, not so demonically cunning as the qualitative desacralization of His sacred humanity and the presentation of a mediocre image of it. The creeping poison which is not noticed until it is too late, is more dangerous than an open attack, than a disease which one recognizes as such as soon as it makes its appearance. The spy is even more dangerous than the enemy who attacks openly.

Everyone can see that the open and emphatic denial of the divinity of Christ is absolutely incompatible with the teaching of the holy Church. This thesis would destroy the basis of the whole Christian Revelation. But this is not so clearly recognized to be the case with the desacralized and mediocre image of the sacred humanity of Christ. The desacralization is introduced under the title of "full humanness" as an orthodox interpretation, and the mediocre image of Jesus is presented under the title of pastoral necessity. Desacralization is not immediately recognized as incompatible with the teaching of the Church. The tendency to undermine the Christian Faith, which is hidden behind it, is not grasped by the faithful. Desacralization is not seen through; it is seen by many as the necessary emphasis on the *"totus homo."* And most children are not able to recognize the mediocre image of Jesus in its radical incompatibility with the Christian Revelation, with the Gospel, if their parents have not already introduced them to the Christian Revelation.

The qualitative distortion of the sacred humanity of Christ certainly has its roots in a lack of faith in the divinity of Christ, in the lack of seriousness with which the substantial union of the human and divine natures is taken. But for the children who are presented with this false, deformed, desacralized humanity, it is the destruction of their faith in the divinity of Christ. The qualitative falsification renders faith impossible for them, for it destroys the Revelation of God in the holy humanity of Christ. It is the cause, and the loss of faith in His divinity is the effect.

Beyond this, the presentation of a mediocre image of Jesus is especially dangerous today because the world as a whole has become much more mediocre than it was, say, 150 years ago. The sense for greatness and depth has completely receded, even on a purely natural[54] level. In the industrialized world which is viewed by Teilhard de Chardin as "progress," in which the machine has replaced the tool and the computer ideal has captivated many people, in which education increases in breadth but loses its depth, in such an age the presentation of a mediocre image of the personality of Christ is harder to recognize for what it is because it fits in so well with our mediocre world. The more our age becomes one in which not only the air is poisoned by chemical elements, but the spiritual and intellectual atmosphere is poisoned by the mass media, the more one brings mediocrity into religion for pastoral reasons.

But the sacred humanity of Christ is not only qualitatively desacralized; the false understanding of *"totus homo"* has disastrous effects in yet another direction. The fact that the Person of Christ, although He possesses a fully human nature, is nevertheless identical with the second Person of the Blessed Trinity, gives the personality of Jesus a unique character. In other words, the mysterious union of divine and human natures in one Person elevates Christ even in His sacred humanity in an inexpressible way above all other men. As the litany of the Sacred Heart, the intimate center of His human nature, says: *"Cor Jesu verbo Dei substan-*

tialiter unitum" ("Heart of Jesus, substantially united to the Word of God"). Even this fundamental truth of the teaching of the holy Church is covered up, thrust as it were into the background by utilizing the *"totus homo"* in order to approach the Man Jesus with doubtful false modern psychological theories. One forgets the essential difference in the humanity of Jesus which is effected by the mysterious "substantial" union with the divine nature. We should never think of Christ, never approach Him, never concern ourselves with the humanity of Christ without keeping before our eyes this dogma, which has been defined *de fide* by the infallible holy Church and is proclaimed in the Nicene Creed:

"Credo . . . et in unum Dominum Jesum Christum, Filium Dei unigenitum. Et ex patre natum ante omnia saecula. Deum de Deo, lumen de lumine, Deum verum de Deo vero. Genitum non factum, consubstantialem Patri: per quem omnia facta sunt. Qui propter nos homines et propter nostram salutem descendit de coelis. Et incarnatus est de Spirtu Sancto . . ."

("I believe in one Lord Jesus Christ, the only-begotten Son of God. Born of the Father before all ages. God of God, light of light, true God of true God. Begotten not made, being of one substance with the Father: by whom all things were made. Who for us men and our salvation came down from heaven. And was made flesh by the Holy Spirit. . . .")

We said before that the qualitative epiphany of God in the holy humanity of Jesus is the basis for our faith in the divinity of Christ, as it was for that of the Apostles. Now we see that the substantial union of the human and divine natures in Jesus Christ is also built into our faith; through the infallible teaching office of the Church we possess the knowledge that it is the second Divine Person who has assumed a human nature in Jesus Christ, as it is clearly stated at the beginning of the Gospel according to St. John: *"Et Verbum caro factum est et habitavit in nobis."* ("And the Word was made flesh, and dwelt among us.")

If we "repress" this and consent to a psychological analysis of the Man Jesus, we have already fallen into a distortion of the figure of Christ, and indeed into apostasy. In addition, the *"totus homo"* in no way contains the claim that the status of Christ, His mission, His holy priesthood, His holy teaching office, His character as King of Kings does not distinguish Him in a unique manner from all mere men, and elevate Him above them. *"Unum est magister vester: Christus"* ("One is your teacher: Christ") : what would be shocking arrogance for any mere man, a demonic pride, is in this case a radiant, blissful truth. In the mouth of Christ, spoken by the Man Jesus, it has a radically different, indeed contrary character to that which it would have in the mouth of any other man, even the most noble, most gifted man. Jesus is the absolute Lord. He issues commandments which are ultimately binding. He absolves sinners from their sins, something which of its very essense God alone can do. He says, "Whoever is not for me is against me." He says on the Cross to the Good Thief, "This day thou shalt be with me in paradise."

But not only are there many things which He alone can say, which in the mouth of any other man would assume a completely different and indeed contrary character, but there are also many things which other men can do, which in the sphere of human life are normal and good, but which are impossible for Christ, because He, as the God-man, is beyond them. Spousal love between man and woman is certainly something which is fundamentally human. It is even something which is especially beautiful and deep. What would human life be if there were no capacity for such a love, or if it could not be actualized? What would human life be if there were no marriage, no generation of children? But nevertheless this would be incompatible with the God-Man Jesus Christ. The notion that the God-Man Jesus Christ would fall in love with a woman and marry her is absurd and conflicts with the unique position of Jesus Christ. This is in no way a limitation of the *"totus homo,"* in no way a lack of perfection of the human nature of the God-Man.

What must be our personal response to this terrible, blasphemous distortion of the sacred humanity of Jesus?

Our first response must be to contemplate the sacred humanity of Jesus Christ in all its inconceivable beauty and holiness. This devilish distortion of the sacred humanity of Christ must lead us to seek *commerce intime* (personal intimacy) with Jesus with renewed zeal. We must steep ourselves in the Scriptures which reveal the holy humanity of Jesus — especially, of course, the Gospels. But the sacred humanity as the epiphany of God, and its substantial union with the second Divine Person of the Blessed Trinity, is illuminated also in the Epistles of Saints Peter and Paul. Yes, in the face of the horrible deformation of the very center of Christian Revelation, we must immerse ourselves in the holy humanity of Christ, contemplating in a special way whatever is filled with the adoration of the God-Man Jesus Christ and which proclaims the sacred humanity of Christ, as do the readings from St. Leo and St. Augustine in the Matins for the feasts of our Lord; as does the hymn of St. Bernard, *Jesus dulcis memoria,* in the Vespers of the feast of the Holy Name of Jesus, and the hymn of Ascension Vespers, *Jesu nostra redemptio.* We must nourish our spirits on books which draw us in a special way into the presence of God (*in conspectu*

Dei) and which proclaim the loving adoration of the sacred humanity of Christ, as the *Confessions* of St. Augustine, the writings of St. Francis of Assisi, the *Philothea* (*Introduction to the Devout Life*) and *Theotimus* of St. Francis de Sales, and many works of Cardinal Newman.

We should build an altar in our hearts for the contemplation of the sacred humanity of Christ and the adoration of the God-Man. And as part of this response we should do penance for the horrible blasphemies which are being perpetuated in catechisms and sermons. And finally, we should battle actively against this distortion and deformation of the holy countenance of Jesus and His sacred humanity, each of us within his own sphere of influence. This battle must be relentless, free from all false, effeminate irenicism.

At the end of this book we will discuss in greater detail the divinely willed response not only to the distortion of the sacred humanity of Christ, but also to the whole devastation of the vineyard of the Lord.

NOTES

49. John Henry Cardinal Newman, *Discourses to Mixed Congregations,* "Purity and Love," p. 69.

50. Preface for Christmas.

51. I have analyzed the unique essence of the person in many of my works. Cf. *Liturgy and Personality, Ethics, Transformation in Christ,* and many essays. Cf. also Josef Seifert, *Erkenntniss objektiver Wahrheit* (Salzburg: Pustet, 1972), and especially his *Leib und Seele* (Salzburg: Pustet, 1973).

52. We want to point out the book by Josef Seifert, *Leib und Seele* (Salzburg: Pustet, 1973), as the most adequate presentation of the true nature of body and soul, of their substantial difference as well as their union in man.

53. We said that the distortion of the sacred humanity of Christ has more the character of a creeping poison than of an open challenge which would deny the divinity of Christ outright. Our main purpose here is to examine the qualitative distortion occurring under the title *"totus homo,"* which even victimizes those who still believe in the divinity of Christ, or

who at least do not dare to deny it. But there are also many who openly express their denial of the divinity of Christ, and for these people this denial is the motive for distorting the sacred humanity of Christ. This is the case, for example, in all the horrible writings of Heer and Holl. However, we are more concerned here with the qualitative distortion of the sacred humanity of Jesus which finds expression in the modern catechisms in America and Europe. It is also found in many plays and musicals, such as *Jesus Christ Superstar,* as well as in all those which, for example, present the relationship between Jesus and Mary Magdalene as a sexual one. The bishops who introduce the false catechisms, or who tolerate such plays, are certainly not all deniers of the divinity of Christ.

15
This-Worldliness

THERE IS A DEEP LINK between the disastrous desacralization of the holy humanity of Christ (which, as emphasized
above, goes together with hatred of the holy and of miracles)
and "this-worldliness" — that is, the transfer of the center
of gravity from eternity to this world.

The glorification of God through our personal sanctification, and — what is more surprising — the salvation of our
souls in eternity, is neglected in favor of improving the world
and fighting poverty and war.

This tendency is especially dangerous and pernicious because, first, it is the basis of many grave errors, and secondly,
because it does not come forth, as other heresies did, as an
explicitly formulated thesis, but as a tacit assumption —
as an inner attitude, a shift of emphasis. As a result, many
of the faithful do not detect its incompatibility with the
Revelation of Christ and the teaching of the Church. Many
Catholics with a deep faith are unwittingly drawn into the

this-worldly attitude, and they just as unwittingly accept the errors which follow from it.

No one presents this-worldliness, and all the errors deriving from it, as a contradiction of the official teaching of the Church. Unlike Karl Rahner's theories on theological pluralism, and Schillebeeckx's denial of any difference between body and soul, these errors are not necessarily linked with an explicit denial of any of the dogmas — and precisely this makes them much more dangerous.

If so many Catholics do not recognize even flagrant contradictions of the teaching of the Church, do not see that clearly irreconcilable things cannot be reconciled, it is not so surprising that they do not see the contradiction to the Church's teaching which lies in tendencies and errors which are not openly proclaimed as incompatible with the dogmas of the Church, but which undermine them mainly by placing a greater emphasis on this world. In this book we mainly want to investigate the tendency in the Church to transfer the center of gravity to this world, as well as the errors connected with this tendency and rooted in it.

The this-worldly tendency can be detected in various pastoral letters, and above all in countless sermons. One speaks more about the fight against poverty and for social justice and world peace — in a word, more about improving the world — than about offending God by our sins, sanctifying the individual, about heaven and hell, eternity and the hope of eternal union with God in the beatific vision.

The this-worldly tendency emphasizes the earthly future more than eternity, and this is an unfortunate heritage of the evolutionism of Teilhard de Chardin. The sanctification of the individual soul and the eternal salvation of the individual is pushed aside to make room for the evolution of mankind on earth, for progress in what concerns man's earthly existence. Against this error we might recall the striking remark of Gustave Thibon: "Je prefère une éternité sans futur à un futur sans éternité." ("I prefer an eternity without future to a future without eternity.")

This-Worldliness: The Wrong Reaction to Distorted Supernaturalism

When we speak of the evil of transferring the center of gravity to this world and to the natural improvement of it, we are not at all speaking of avoiding a certain false supernaturalism. There have been Catholics who, believing that the primacy of the supernatural demands indifference to all earthly sufferings, have fallen into a false zeal and become hard and inhuman. As long as such Catholics heard only of great earthly sufferings and of heavy crosses inflicted on their neighbor, they remained indifferent. They awakened toward their neighbor only if he was in danger of offending God by a sin and thus endangering his eternal salvation. They were then ready to make great sacrifices to prevent the offense to God and to help their neighbor to return to Him.

This was a harsh attitude which contradicted the spirit of true charity; it was a pseudo-supernaturalism. To observe the right hierarchy of things, does not mean ignoring all those goods which are beneath the highest good. If we feel no sympathy with the sufferings of our neighbor or even of someone personally dear to us, simply because his eternal salvation is not endangered by his suffering, then we have fallen into an unchristian hardness of heart, a betrayal of charity, a repulsive fanaticism. This false supernaturalism in reality treats the glorification of God and eternal salvation as a merely natural "ideal" and no longer understands their true supernatural character. We will see later on how all genuine goods, including all natural ones, are established in their true importance by the perspective of the supernatural goods and their primacy. Only in the light of Christ can a genuine good display its true nature — this holds for a real evil as well. As the Psalmist says: "In lumine tuo videbimus lumen." ("in Your light we see light.")

It is a regrettable sophism to say (as it was said sometimes in sermons) that the death of a father or mother, husband or wife, or of a child, is no reason for sadness as long as they died well, after receiving the last sacraments, as long as we can hope that they are with God. Of course the eternal happiness of one whom we truly love is the most important thing, but separation from the beloved, even if only for a time, remains a terrible cross. Whoever does not feel this cross, whoever just happily goes his way with the consolation that the beloved has found eternal blessedness, is not directed to eternity in a special way — he is simply insensitive and does not want to be disturbed in the normal rhythm of his daily life. He is simply making a comfortable excuse when he emphasizes that the eternal salvation of the other is the most important thing. He has forgotten that even Jesus Christ, the God-man, prayed in Gethsemane: "Father, if it be possible, let this cup pass from me." He does not understand that a cross which has been imposed on us should be suffered under as a cross. Only then can we attain to the true consolation which lies in the perspective of eternity, to the true hope of eternal blessedness.

We should simply read the magnificent sermon of St. Bernard of Clairvaux (no. 26 in his sermons on the Canticle of Canticles) in which he grieves over the death of his brother. Here we find first of all the lamentation, filled with deep grief, over the death of his beloved brother, and only then the ascent to the fact that death is the beginning of a life of eternal blessedness.

It is always a disastrous mistake when we try to skip over certain phases instead of passing through them, when we violate the central virtue of *discretio*. (I have spoken at length about this virtue in my book, *Liturgy and Personality*.) When we do not pass through the necessary phases on our way to some end, phases which are objectively prescribed by the nature of things, and are willed by God, when we try to skip them, then we distort everything and do not really attain to our end; in fact, we falsify the end and render it mediocre.

If we possess real charity then the physical suffering of our neighbor must move us deeply. We have to try to mitigate his suffering as much as we can. Consider the importance of curing the sick in the life of Christ! Of course, these cures, being miraculous, were also meant to reveal the divinity of Christ. But at the same time they show the divine mercy, the triumphant love of Jesus for men. Consider, too, the importance of miraculous cures in the lives of so many saints. A missionary who would say, "I am only interested in the conversion of the pagans; whether they are starving, or suffering terrible diseases, doesn't interest me," would be a traitor to the spirit of Christ. The true missionary does not at all become indifferent to earthly sufferings simply because he clearly realizes that the conversion of men is an incomparably higher good than health or the mitigation of inhuman poverty. In fact, he becomes especially alert to the earthly sufferings of his neighbor through the light and spirit of Christ and His holy Church. For it belongs to the nature of true charity that, precisely from the perspective of the true hierarchy of goods and of the absolute primacy of the good of eternal salvation, it is deeply interested in all objective goods for the person of the neighbor, and of course in the elimination of all objective evils for him. The greater this holy love of charity is, the more differentiated it is! This is shown in the lives of the saints. And have we forgotten which miracle was the first which Jesus worked? Have we forgotten that at the wedding feast of Cana it was a natural evil that was eliminated: "They have no more wine."

"The first miracle of our Lord, at the wedding feast of Cana, is one of the three mysteries which is celebrated at Epiphany. The Gospel says, 'He revealed His glory, and His disciples believed in Him.' The Church sees in this miracle primarily the revelation of the divinity of Christ. But it is at the same time a revelation of the boundless superabundance of divine love. The first miracle of Jesus was neither the cure of a sick person, nor the restoration of some great natural good, such as sight to the man born blind; it did not even involve some indispensable good, as the multiplication of loaves. The transformation of water into wine was not strictly indispensable either for the married couple or for the wedding feast. It only served to heighten the joy of the festive occasion. And it is not as if there was no wine at all, there was just not enough. O divine superfluity! Christ our Savior, who constantly admonishes us to seek 'the one thing necessary,' is greatly concerned that the joy of the wedding feast be undisturbed, and that the groom not be embarrassed because of a lack of wine!"[55]

It must be said emphatically: the opposite of this-worldliness is not a pseudo-supernaturalism which dehumanizes a man and makes him indifferent and insensitive to the earthly sufferings of his neighbor, and even to his own sufferings, as well as to the natural goods which God sends him and which confer happiness on him. No, the true antithesis to the disastrous this-worldliness is the attitude of the saints. Precisely because of their primary concern with the "one thing necessary," because of their love of Christ, their "I-Thou" communion with Jesus, their *commerce intime* with Him, they were filled with that true charity which sympathizes with the sufferings of our neighbor, which works for the relief of his sufferings in a way which differs utterly from all merely humanitarian love. Love of neighbor is really possible only when the primacy of the love of God is observed; and the saint, far from losing his true humanity, attains to a supernaturally transfigured humanity.

Insidious Distortion of Revelation by Wrong Emphasis rather than Formal Heresy

Now we have to show that a distortion of the notion of salvation is linked with this preoccupation with the earthly progress of mankind. The Catholic teaching on justification is pushed aside. It is not that one wants to accept the Protestant *sola fides* (faith alone justifies) teaching out of an ill-conceived ecumenism towards Protestants (though such ill-conceived ecumenism is found in many areas today). One rather over-emphasizes the teaching that all men, whether they are Catholic, Christian, or pagan, can attain to eternal blessedness. I speak of an overemphasis, because the teaching that all men can be saved through the mercy of God if they lead a life corresponding to the highest norms which they know of, was defined by the First Vatican Council. But today the notion of sin is explained away by many, and hell is hardly mentioned any more in catechisms and sermons.

I am not speaking here of a direct denial of the most fundamental elements of the Christian revelation and of the dogmas of the holy Church. What is at stake is whether the basic truths of the Faith are treated in a way which is appropriate in the light of the whole of Revelation.[56] Today we find a silence about certain dogmas, a shift in the center of gravity: a lack of interest in what belongs to the essence of Christian revelation, in favor of things which are related at most only as indirect consequences to the mission of the Church, which is the sanctification and salvation of souls. The improvement of the earthly lot of mankind — the elimination of poverty and war — is surely a thing of great natural value, and interest in this is a praiseworthy moral attitude. But is this what Christ came for, is this why the second divine Person took on human nature? What is the worth of all external improvement of human life when compared to the fact that in baptism a new and divine principle of life is conferred on man which opens to him the possibility of sanctification, of glorifying God, of eternal blessedness? Indeed, a world in which there were no more poverty, no more wars, and even no more disease — a world without physical and psychic suffering — *would have no right to exist even for a moment, and would be worthy of sinking into nothingness if no one in it bowed his knee before Christ, if no one worshipped God.*

With this background we have to ask: in the Church today, in pastoral letters and sermons, does one not speak much more of earthly improvement than of incomparably more important things such as our redemption through Christ's death on the cross, the communication of supernatural life, the sanctification of the individual, the resulting glorification of God, and eternal blessedness?

Some of the Arguments Used to Defend This-Worldliness

Now many persons will object: the Church has spoken about these things for two thousand years, but is it not something both beautiful and necessary that she finally begins to take seriously the natural evils under which men suffer, and earthly destitution? Is this not one of the great achievements of Vatican II, that the Church has left her ghetto and has actively committed herself to the mitigation of human needs in all areas of life? Is this not a consequence of genuine love of neighbor?

To this we respond: it is totally untrue to say that the Church before Vatican II was not interested in the earthly needs of mankind. Have those people who are constantly singing the praises of history, who speak as if history were a source of God's revelation, who look upon it as the ultimate reality, have they really so little knowledge of history, are they really such ignoramuses with regard to history, that they do not know what the various orders of the Church have achieved towards the mitigation of the earthly needs of man? Do they not know that all hospitals were once both founded and directed by religious orders, and that there are orders which were founded specifically for this work, such as the Fathers of Mercy? That it was certain orders which founded the "Monti di Pietà" for the relief of poverty? That there was an order of Trinitarians founded to ransom Christian slaves from the Moslems? Have they heard nothing of the help which St. Vincent de Paul provided for the poor, nothing of the Society of St. Vincent of Paul founded by the blessed Ozanam? Do these people not know how urgently the Church, in Pope Leo XIII's *Rerum Novarum*, called for opposition to the excesses of capitalism, and to social injustice? Have they forgotten Pope Benedict XV's repeated call for peace and an end to the First World War? Do they know nothing of the encyclical *Quadragesimo Anno*?

But, above all, we have to emphasize the following: the

primary sphere of love of neighbor is the individual neighbor. The relief of his earthly suffering and needs is clearly essential to this love. This plays a central role in the Gospel — think of the parable of Lazarus and Dives. But working for charitable institutions is a much less immediate expression of love of neighbor. This is much more indirectly linked with love of neighbor than when one personally and individually helps some poor person. Giving of alms has in all eras been regarded as an essential duty of the true Christian, and indeed has been required by the Church. But a mere financial contribution to a charitable organization is much more impersonal than helping one's individual neighbor. Such a contribution reaches some unknown person only indirectly, and the fact that it goes through an impersonal organization makes it a much more indirect expression of love of neighbor. This, of course, is in no way to deny the value of such contributions.

But someone will object: We should not only be concerned with the needs of other men and with the destitution which befalls many, such as starvation in a catastrophe. The progressivists in the Church argue that we should also take up the struggle against poverty by reorganizing the political structure of the state; we should fight against the social injustice which prevails in many countries; we should not only give alms, no, we should work for a state of things in which everyone can lead a human existence, in which all involuntary poverty is eliminated. And besides, it is argued, almsgiving tends to make what is a response to the demands of justice, appear to be an act of loving pity.

Much could be said by way of response to this point of view, and we cannot here assume the task of saying it all. Social justice is undoubtedly of high value. But this justice demands only that a worker be rightly paid, that his wage correspond to his achievement in work. It demands that the worker be treated in a decent human way, that he never be exploited, that he be regarded primarily as a human person and never merely as a worker — and above all, it demands that he never be made a mere means for something. Social justice does not demand the elimination of poverty, though the Christian should nevertheless try to eliminate squalid poverty.

The elimination of social injustice can to a great extent be brought about only by state laws, and this is something which lies neither in the power of the holy Church, nor of the individual. And besides, such a change of state laws does not belong to the specific mission of the holy Church. It belongs to the real mission of the Church to defend morality, to admonish men to it, to impose it upon every individual Christian, and this involves fighting the moral evil which everyone commits who commits a social injustice. The Church must oppose this injustice as a sin because, like all sins, it offends God and endangers the eternal salvation of the man who commits the sin. But it is only indirectly her task to obtain a more just order of things in the state.

Of course it is also a task of the Church, and a matter of social justice, to admonish the state to form its constitution according to the principles of justice. And the Church has repeatedly made such admonitions: I mention here only *Rerum Novarum* of Leo XIII, and *Quadragesimo Anno* of Pius XI. And as soon as moral and basic philosophical issues come up, especially in the political sphere, the Church should intervene in the most effective way, admonishing and exhorting, as Pius XI did in his encyclicals, *Mit brennender Sorge,* and *On Atheistic Communism.* This voice of the

Church is unfortunately ignored by the atheistic and Communist states, and this means that it is not superfluous to renew the condemnation of Communism.

It is an old error to say that the Church should not get involved in politics, that this is not her domain. Of course, this is not her immediate task, and her influence depends on many factors. But that does not change the fact that she must take a stand as soon as ultimate questions come up in politics. During my fight against Nazism, I wrote in my newspaper, *Der Christliche Ständestaat*: "The Church should not be politicized, but politics should be Catholicized."

Nevertheless it remains true that the primary task of the Church is the proclamation of the divine Revelation, the protection of it against all heresies, the sanctification of the soul of the individual, the securing of his eternal salvation — this is the spreading of the kingdom of God on earth, and not the attempt to build up an earthly paradise.

It is still more important to see that the motive of many for eliminating poverty (which itself is not morally wicked, but only a morally relevant evil) is not rooted in the spirit of Christ and His gospel, but in a humanitarian ideal. The widespread tendency today to demand everything as a right and to refuse to accept any gifts is surely no manifestation of a Christian spirit. There is in reality a clear, sharply delineated difference between justice and love. Justice can and should be protected and demanded by state law; but love of neighbor could never be demanded by any law. For it is a duty before God, and no state law ever could or should prescribe it or enforce it. Love of neighbor presupposes the fulfillment of the claims of justice, but it goes far beyond this. The words of the gospel, "if someone asks you to go one mile, go two miles with him," clearly go far beyond the sphere of justice.

Of course, it is pharisaical hypocrisy to fulfill the demands of justice as if one were giving alms. But it is terrible pride not to want to accept any alms, and to demand that which comes as a gift. The true Christian should be happier to receive alms and to be grateful for them, than simply to receive what he has a right to. When he receives a gift he is happy not only over the good which is the gift, but also over the goodness of the giver; and he experiences it as a great source of happiness that he can and should be grateful.

It is definitely no part of the message of Christ that there is to be no more poverty, no more war, that the earth is to become a natural paradise. But a deep interest in the earthly welfare of our neighbor is a central duty of the Christian and an essential demand of the love of neighbor.

It remains true, however, that the shift of emphasis which was our starting point in this chapter, the emphasizing of the natural improvement of the world at the expense of the glorification of God, of the sanctification and eternal beatitude of man, is a disastrous confusion.

NOTES

54. By "natural" we do not of course mean here "effortless" or "spontaneous"; rather, we mean, as is clear from the context of this sentence: pertaining to that realm which is precisely distinguished from the supernatural.

55. From my book, *The Sacred Heart* (Baltimore: Helicon, 1965), p. 124.

56. This distortion which comes from false emphases has been discussed by Bishop Graber, *op. cit.*, in the chapter, "Kryptograme Haeresie." As he shows, this phrase was coined by Karl Rahner, who wrote in 1961: cryptogrammic heresy is present "when for instance one scrupulously avoids speaking of hell, when one no longer speaks of the evangelical counsels, of the meaning of vows or of life in a religious order, or when one speaks with hesitation and embarrassment about these things if some mention of them cannot be avoided. When a preacher is speaking to an

educated congregation today, how often does he preach to them about temporal punishment for sins, about indulgences, about angels, fasting, the devil (the preacher might at the most still say something about the 'demonic' in man), purgatory, prayer for the poor souls, and similar supposedly outmoded things." And Rahner adds quite rightly that cryptogrammic heresy commonly goes hand in hand with "explicit orthodoxy." From Rahner's "A New Form of Heresy," in *Nature and Grace* (New York, Sheed and Ward, 1964), pp. 75-6.

57. An encyclical addressed to the German people in their own language and smuggled into the country in 1937. It is a condemnation of national-socialism and also treats more generally of philosophical, political, and juridical theories. It is noted especially for its precise definition of natural law.

16

Distortion of Morality and of Love of Neighbor

THIS SHIFT OF EMPHASIS is also expressed in a distortion of morality. First of all, morality is stripped of its transcendence and reduced to relations among men. One fails to see that all morality unfolds between God and man. Even if in many sins we do wrong to other men, the moral evil of the wrong, the moral disvalue of our behavior, is always directed against God. God is offended by sin. The wrong which I do another can be forgiven me by him; but the sin, the moral evil of my behavior, can only be forgiven me by God. I am responsible to God for the sin. The transcendence of moral good and evil, which points beyond this world and our earthly existence into eternity, is related to the fact that the drama of moral good and evil unfolds between God and man.

Secondly, one distorts morality by reducing it to love of neighbor. We have already mentioned that many sins are immediately directed against God and that they lie outside of the sphere of love of neighbor: for example, the sin of pride — the *non serviam* (I will not serve) of Lucifer, the sin of impurity, the sin of lying (even if it does not involve any deception which harms another), the sin of disobeying the positive commands of God. Furthermore, there are sins which are based on a wrong which I inflict on myself. Suicide is only a wrong against myself, not against another, unless there are special circumstances. But the immorality of suicide, the sin of it, is directed, as in every sin, against God. The sin of me playing Lord of life and death, of arrogating a right which I do not possess, is committed in euthanasia, in which I perhaps even do good to a suffering person. If even a deed which does another person good can be morally wrong, can be a sin offending God, then it is clear that morality cannot be reduced to love of neighbor, and even less to human relations.

A distortion of love of neighbor goes together with this distortion of morality. The very expression in German, *Mitmenschlichkeit,* shows the humanitarian perversion of love of neighbor. This perversion comes mainly from the separation of love of neighbor from its root in the love of Christ. Here, too, this separation is not put forward as an explicit, heretical thesis. We are not here speaking of the patently foolish statements of those priests and laymen who say: if atheists have neglected the love of God, they have cultivated the love of neighbor, whereas Christians have neglected the love of neighbor in cultivating the love of God; Christians and atheists must, then, learn from one another, and complement one another. This is sheer nonsense. But here we are speaking of an insidious poison, of tendencies which, by false emphases or by silence on certain truths, undermine the substance of the Christian revelation and the teaching of the holy Church.[58]

This subversion of Christian truth occurs when love of

neighbor is said to be the *only* actualization of the love of Christ, or when love of neighbor is said to be identical with the love of God in and through Christ.

Love of neighbor is indeed a necessary fruit of the true love of God. If there is no love of neighbor, there is no true love of God. Love of neighbor is a test for the authenticity and the extent of our love of God. But it is by no means the only manifestation or actualization of the love of God.

The fact that one thing is a test for the presence of another, does not mean that this thing is the only manifestation and actualization of it. Whether a man is honest is surely a test for his moral standing. If someone is dishonest and is deceitful in small things, it perhaps reveals that his whole moral character is bad. But this does not mean that honesty is the only manifestation of a man's moral attitudes, nor that it is their only possible actualization. Consider how the love of God in and through Christ manifests itself apart from love of neighbor. Consider every deep repentance over our sins; consider all the virtues, especially purity and humility, as well as acts of adoration of God, acts of obedience toward the positive commands of God and His holy Church. The love of God shows itself in resisting temptations to do something morally wrong, in obeying God rather than man, in resisting public opinion, in being free from human respect, and in countless other attitudes which are not forms of love of neighbor. But the highest manifestations of love of God, the highest actualization of love of Christ, the deed which reaches beyond every other moral deed and attains to sanctity, is the death of a martyr, which can obviously not be interpreted as a fruit of love of neighbor. In the whole Christian tradition martyrdom has held the highest place, and every martyr has been numbered among the saints on the basis of his martyrdom.

But above all there is a full actualization of love of Christ when we respond directly to the incomprehensible holiness of Jesus by showing Him adoring love and loving adoration. When we examine our conscience and awaken repentance in ourselves, there is an actualization of the love of God — we direct ourselves immediately to God, we accuse ourselves before Him, and feel the pain of having offended Him: now all this is a pure manifestation of the love of God.

We find a special manifestation of this love in the contemplative adoration of Christ, in the *commerce intime* with Jesus, such as we find in mystics, like St. Catherine of Siena. The importance of the direct love of Christ in her dialogues with Jesus, should make it clear what the actualization of this direct love is, and what a sublime value it possesses. But of course this direct love of Jesus is in no way limited to the mystics.

All this shows clearly how nonsensical it is to make the even more radical statement that love of neighbor is not only the one possible manifestation of love of God, but that they are both identical. In this thesis the nature of love of God and love of Christ is utterly misunderstood. One no longer sees that this love is a unique value response to the infinite holiness of God and of Christ, one no longer understands the nature of this love and its difference from any kind of love for a creature. One has thereby ceased to understand the center, the soul of the Christian Faith. One has simply eliminated the first of Christ's two greatest commandments ("You shall love the Lord your God with your whole heart, with your whole mind, with your whole strength") and pretends that there is only the second of the two commandments. This is surely the most catastrophic of all the consequences of this-worldliness and of the shift of emphasis which we discussed above.

Essential Difference between Love of God and Love of Neighbor, and the Relation between Them

In my book *Das Wesen der Liebe* (The Nature of Love), I have dealt at length with the radical difference in kind between love of God and love of neighbor. Here I limit myself to certain points developed in the eleventh chapter of that book. The love for God and for Christ, the God-man, is the adoring love of the creature, it is a love in which I ultimately abandon my very being to the Lord. It would be idolatrous blasphemy to show this love for any creature, and in reality this would not even be possible.

This deep qualitative difference is expressed in the formulation of the two great commandments. The first is: "You shall love the Lord your God with your whole heart, with your whole mind, with your whole strength." But the second is formulated this way: "Love your neighbor as yourself."

Furthermore, the love for God and for Jesus is a value response *par excellence,* whereas in the love of neighbor we approach and embrace our neighbor with a holy goodness which, as we shall see, is exclusively a fruit of the love for God and for Christ. The love of neighbor, which we should show even to an odious and repulsive man, indeed, even to an enemy of God, is not awakened and motivated by the beauty of the neighbor. A pure value response toward the character of such men would rather have to be the radical rejection of them. It is only the holy goodness which unfolds in our love for Christ and which, having received the seeds of it in baptism, we show toward such men despite their disvalues — it is only this which enables us to see the ontological value which each of them possesses as *imago Dei* (image of God), and to see the sacred dignity which each possesses because Christ died on the Cross for him.

As a further fundamental difference between love of neighbor and love for Christ, let us add that the love for Christ brings with it the yearning to be united with Him who is infinitely holy. In this love the *intentio unionis* (desire for union with the beloved) is in the foreground, whereas in the love of neighbor this *intentio unionis* plays a much smaller role than the *intentio benevolentiae* (desire to confer good upon the beloved). The love for God and for Christ is more similar to marital love than to love of neighbor, as far as the prominence of the *intentio unionis* goes. This point of similarity is the basis of many analogies in the liturgy, and is expressed in the language of the mystics. The love for Christ, the loving adoration and contemplation of Him, is an infinite source of happiness, a climax of *frui* (contemplative enjoyment). But none of this is found in love of neighbor or love of enemy — this love is a source of happiness only in the very different way that through it we dwell in the kingdom of holy goodness. The "beloved," he to whom we show love of neighbor, is not a source of happiness, but rather the union with Christ which is actualized in the love of neighbor is the source of happiness.

When one emphasizes the dependency of love of neighbor on love for Christ, these words of Christ are quite often cited as an objection: "Whatever you have done to the least of my brethren, you have done to me." In *The Trojan Horse in the City of God* I have dealt with the misunderstanding which is at the basis of this objection. But I want to take up the matter again, since this misunderstanding is so widespread.

In these words, love of Christ, direct response to Him, as well as loving obedience, are presupposed. For we would all be ready to help Christ if we should encounter Him personally. The fact that love for Christ is presupposed, is clearly shown when, after Christ speaks the surprising words, "I was hungry, and you did not give me to eat, naked, and you did not cloth me," He is then asked, "Lord, when did we see You hungry, and not give You to eat?" By Christ identifying Himself with the least of His brothers, a link is established between the deed of love of neighbor, and the love for Christ. This gives us a totally new motivation for loving our neighbor. But this link in no way involves any identification of love of neighbor and love for God. This encounter with Christ in the least of men is something wonderful, something mysterious — but what is found is not the individual character of such men, not their value, but rather the merciful love of Christ, the embrace of His love. Thus the sense in which He is present in our neighbor in no way eliminates the infinite difference between the sacred humanity of Christ and all other men.

Someone might object: what has been said holds only for bad men who neglect their neighbor and who excuse themselves by saying that they have not neglected Him; but how are we to understand the words of Christ to the good, "You fed me when I was hungry, you clothed me when I was naked." These, too, answer, "Lord, when did we feed you and cloth you?" Do we not have here a finding of Christ in our neighbor? If Christ can say, "What you have done to the least of my brethren, you have done to me," then the good deeds done for our neighbor refer to Christ, even if they were done with reference to our neighbor rather than to Christ.

But to all this we have to say that even here there is no

question of finding Christ in our neighbor. This is shown in their answer, "Lord, when did we meet you and feed you?" What they did was to follow the commandments of Christ. Christ, who has said, "Whoever loves me keeps my commandments," has enjoined love of neighbor upon us. But following His commandments — a clear consequence of loving Christ — is obviously quite different from finding Christ in our neighbor. The radical difference in kind, and even the qualitative difference, between the love for Christ and the love of neighbor is in no way blurred.

Furthermore, we have to distinguish here between two different meanings of "find." It can mean that someone, such as a saint, can somehow disclose to us the reality of Christ. In this sense, as we will see, we do not find Christ in our neighbor. But if we take "find" in the sense of "encounter," then there is a meaning to the statement that we find Christ in our neighbor. But this encounter with Him has quite a special character; it is radically different from every direct contact with Christ. When we turn to Christ in prayer, and when he touches our heart in a special way, this contact has a completely different character from every encounter with Him in our neighbor. This contact is the source of the highest and most sublime happiness which we can experience on earth (unless we receive mystical graces), for the vision of Jesus face to face in eternity will be the source of our blessedness. This personal contact with Christ is the real finding of Him — and Jesus delights and intoxicates our souls, and fills them with happiness.

We find a distant analogy in the case of a saint, who reflects the infinite holiness of Christ. But this is not at all true of our neighbor. Only as a fruit of loving Christ, in the realization that Christ, too, loves our neighbor, in the knowledge that He has said, "What you have done to the least of my brothers, you have done to me," only thus can we attain to true love of neighbor and encounter Christ in our neighbor, see him in the light of Christ. Then we find in him, not exactly Christ, but a preciousness and loveableness which he has through Christ, as one sent and loved by Him. So we see that even the words of Jesus addressed to the good, "What you have done to the least of my brothers, you have done to me," in no way blurs the radical difference in kind and the qualitative difference between love for Christ and love of neighbor. We can never experience Christ in our neighbor, and the response of love to Christ makes love of neighbor possible in the first place.

We repeat: we can never experience Christ in our neighbor. Our neighbor is in no way an "epiphany" of God — he does not disclose to us an incomprehensible holiness — he is a man with all his weaknesses, and sometimes laden with terrible disvalues. *Qua* neighbor he has no qualitative similarity with Jesus at all. Thus the finding of Christ in our neighbor involves no revelation of the sacred humanity of Christ, nor any response to a reflection of His sacred humanity. We can see this clearly in comparing our love for a neighbor with the love which a saint can engender in our hearts. The saint is a reflection of Jesus, he has a qualitative similarity with the sacred humanity of Jesus, he is an imitation of Christ, however great the difference which remains between him and Christ. In the saint we can discover something of the unique quality of holiness. He is thus in his holiness a way for us to reach Christ. Reverent love for him contains a weak analogy to our love for Christ. This love, which for instance Brother Leo felt for St. Francis of Assisi, is a pure value response.

In order to meet Christ in our neighbor, especially in the suffering and the needy, we have to have already found Christ and have given a value response to His infinite holiness. Here "find" means that we see in our neighbor someone who is loved and redeemed by Christ, and that we know that we should treat him as such. Love of neighbor is a command of Christ, and there is a link in Matthew 25 between our relation to our neighbor and our relation to Christ, because Christ has said, "Whoever loves me keeps my commandments." Every act of love of neighbor is a glorification of God, as is all supernatural morality, and every manifestation of love of neighbor refers ultimately to Christ.

It is not as if love of neighbor were only an act of obedience to Christ. That would be a great error, against which I have written in many of my works (especially *The Sacred Heart,* and the chapter "False Reactions" in *The Trojan Horse*).[59] No, love of neighbor implies a real interest in our neighbor as such, as this unrepeatable unique individual. But real love of neighbor demands the love of Christ, which precedes the love of neighbor and is radically different from it. It demands holy goodness in our souls, and the direct love for Jesus of which it is constituted. Only in direct, loving confrontation with Christ can He let this holy goodness, which is the essence of caritas, unfold in our souls. It belongs to the nature of love of neighbor that we approach our neighbor with this holy goodness, even before we have responded to him individually. And only through love for Christ, only through the freeing of our vision by direct value response to Him, can we discover in our neighbor — despite all his ugliness, his mediocrity, his hostility to God — the ontological value which he possesses as *imago Dei* (image of God), a value which cannot be destroyed as long as a man lives, not even by himself.[60]

Here we have to mention the particular loveableness of those who suffer; this is something which not every one who is our neighbor possesses. The suffering which a man has to bear is a cross which God has imposed on him. All suffering which has the character of a cross confers a certain aura on him who suffers — it is something which should fill us with a certain reverence. Through Christ and in Christ all suffering and all crosses have become something honorable.

There is of course a noble pity which is purely natural and which presupposes neither the Christian Revelation nor the love of Christ. There is a humanitarian love of man, and much good has been done for men as a result of this pity and a natural readiness to help. But as I have shown at length in my book, *Das Wesen der Liebe* (The Nature of Love), these attitudes are radically different from Christian love of neighbor. True love of neighbor necessarily presupposes, as we have shown above, direct love for Christ, a value response to His sacred humanity and to the self-revelation of God in Him, and this is something radically different from humanitarian love of neighbor.

It is bad enough that one distorts the love of neighbor by failing to understand that it is rooted in the pure love for Jesus; it is bad enough that, caught up in a false this-worldliness, one is more concerned with one's neighbor than with obeying, loving, and glorifying God. But in addition to all this we cannot fail to recognize the materialism which lies in the fact that one emphasizes mainly that love of neighbor which refers to material goods. In sermons and even in pastoral letters we constantly hear about the struggle against poverty and war — but little about spiritual goods for our neighbor and about that burning zeal for his salvation which consumed all the saints and all *homines religiosi* (religious men).

We have already mentioned that real love of neighbor finds its highest expression in an interest in his sanctification and eternal salvation. But here we want to mention some of the expressions of true love of neighbor. It is for instance love of neighbor to console in their worries those lonely persons who are not supported by any human love, to surround them with human warmth; to listen patiently to our neighbor, to sympathize with him in his psychic and spiritual sufferings, to be patient with him, to rejoice with him in his happiness, to stimulate him intellectually, to disclose values to him in the realm of beauty, to disclose truths to him; to give him the spiritual help he needs to come closer to Jesus; and there are many, many other ways of showing love of neighbor.

What we have said here about the relation between love of God and love of neighbor, has always been understood in the Church. What was the main theme in the writings of the great theologians and mystics? Whether we look to the *Confessions* of St. Augustine, to the *Itinerarium* (The Journey of the Soul to God) of St. Bonaventure, to the *Dialogue* of St. Catherine of Siena, to the writings of St. Theresa of Avila or St. John of the Cross, to the *Theotimus* of St. Francis de Sales, or to the many writings of the great Cardinal Newman —in all these works we will find in the foreground the love of God, the love for Jesus Christ, although love of neighbor as a necessary fruit of love for God is done full justice. In all of them we find the intimate relation between the two loves clearly stated — but each is always in the right

hierarchical relation to the other, and the two are never iden-
tified.

But today? Where are the theologians who still speak of
the direct love for God, of the *commerce intime* with Jesus?
What sermons, pastoral letters, or encyclicals deal exten-
sively with the nature of the direct love for God, for Christ
Jesus, and with the difference between this love and love of
neighbor, and with the way in which love of neighbor is
grounded in love for God?

How Neglect of Love for God Leads to Distortion of Love of Neighbor

The distortion of the sacred humanity of Jesus, of which
we spoke above, and the resulting failure to understand the
love for Christ (we have said that this love is the axis of
sanctification and of the whole Christian life) also necessarily
leads to a distortion and watering down of the love of neighbor itself. One sign of this distortion is the cry for peace
which can be heard everywhere in the Church, and the failure
to remember that Christ not only said that He came to bring
peace, but also that He came to bring the sword (Mt. 10:34).

Love of neighbor is confused with a cheerful willingness to
give in. One no longer understands that real love of neighbor
just as often has to say "No" to the wishes of our neighbor as
"Yes." Through the disastrous shift of emphasis which lies in
this-worldliness, one has lost sight of the great drama of human existence — the fall of man, his redemption by Christ,
the fact that justification calls for sanctification, the responsibility which we have as a result, the fact that this life is a
status viae (a pilgrimage), that we face the alternatives of
eternal blessedness and damnation, of heaven and hell. True
love of neighbor demands that we be awakened to this drama;
our unique interest in him is possible only when we see him

in the light of this drama. Love of neighbor is impossible in the presence of mediocrity, of the repulsiveness of evil pride, of the deadly oppressive atmosphere of an enemy of God like Hitler, unless we see our neighbor in the light of the objective tragedy which these attitudes involve. Then we see in our neighbor a man who was created in the image of God, called by God to *similitudo Dei* in personal sanctification and to eternal union with God, but who has brought the most terrible guilt upon himself, who is facing the terrible judgment of God, who has rejected the redeeming hand of Christ. Only in this supernatural light, against the background of this tragedy, is it possible to show him true love of neighbor. As soon as we lose sight of the supernatural situation of man and see everything in the light of this world, it not only becomes impossible to show love of neighbor toward the enemy of God, but this love is deprived of all its power and depth.

No sooner has one forgotten that the eternal salvation of our neighbor has to be our main concern for him, than real love of neighbor becomes impossible. No sooner does one cease to understand that love of neighbor does not seek fulfilment of all his wishes, than this love becomes a weakness and a way of giving in. No sooner does one forget the words of St. Augustine, *"Interficere errorem, diligere errantem"* ("kill the error, love him who errs"), than one loses all understanding for real love of neighbor. Love of neighbor can only be rightly understood when we realize that we live in a situation in which we are bound to reject all moral mistakes and even many non-moral disvalues, in which we have to struggle against error and evil — struggle against them with all our might — but in which love of neighbor extends even to him who errs, who is evil, even to him who is the enemy of

God. We can understand love of neighbor rightly, and its holy power, only when we see it against the background of all those acts which reject what is wrong. To this we are called, indeed obliged.

The Mysteries of the Faith Interpreted as a Means for Love of Neighbor

Some Catholics who indeed believe in the dogmas but who are primarily concerned with the improvement of the world, regard the Incarnation, the Redemption, sanctifying grace, all as *means* for the growth of love of neighbor. (They express this not so much in an explicit statement as in their attitudes.) Fraternal charity seems to them the goal for the sake of which God does everything that He does. They no longer see the incomprehensible glory of the Incarnation as such, this manifestation of the infinite love and mercy of God, and fall down in adoration. They no longer see the ultimate seriousness of the economy of Redemption — the horror of being separated from God, the *in umbra mortis sedere* (sitting in the shadow of death), and then the tremendous source of all true joy, the Redemption through Christ, of which the Church sings at Easter: *"Agnus redemit oves: Christus innocens Patri reconciliavit peccatores"* ("The lamb has redeemed the sheep: Christ who was innocent has reconciled sinners to the Father"). The Redemption makes the eternal happiness of the individual possible, and this is incomparably more important than any earthly progress.

When we say that such Catholics fail to understand the tremendous gift of sanctifying grace, which makes it possible for us to become holy and thus — and this is the most important thing of all — to glorify God, they would protest that they do believe all this. But the proof that they have fallen prey to this-worldliness is their unconscious tendency to look upon all this as a means, and to set as their main goal fraternal charity and earthly peace.

In this way one becomes blind even to the real glory and specific value of love of neighbor. For as we saw, this love is possible only as a fruit of our love for Jesus Christ; by its nature it flows from a love very different in kind, from love for Christ and for God in and through Christ. This love cannot be compared with any love for a creature. It is a value-response to God's incomprehensible holiness.

Love of neighbor is no longer understood in its specific value, and as a glorification of God; instead, one sees mainly its effect in improving the world. This is a particularly dangerous form of this-worldliness, because here the objective hierarchy of things is totally reversed, and one falls into a kind of religious utilitarianism without at all understanding its incompatibility with the teaching of the Church.

NOTES

58. "Today one does not try to lead man to Christ, rather Christ is reduced to the merely human and the social. Christ has indeed sent us pastors to men, but this was so that we might lead them to Him, so that they might through Him receive grace and come to the Father." Quoted in *Una Voce Korrespondenz*, Januar/Februar, 1972, from the letter of a Lutheran pastor to a Roman Catholic priest.

59. However grave this error, it is a lesser error than today's tendency to reduce love of God to love of neighbor, as the following consideration will show:

In every case in which one identifies different things, there is a very great difference, according to the "direction" which the identification takes. For example, the identification of body and soul can take the form of reducing the soul to the body (materialism), or of reducing the body to the soul and thus denying the full reality of matter (as in Berkeley's spiritualism). Similarly, there is a great difference between the pantheism which divinizes nature, and the pantheism which makes God a part of nature, that is, which naturalizes Him.

The "direction" of an identification is something different from the error of the identification itself, from the error of identifying different things.

It is a fundamental error not to distinguish body and soul. But prescinding from this error, there is the question whether in this identification one denies the body and matter, or the soul and spirit. This latter is by far the graver error. Thus today in the Church when one identifies love of God with love of neighbor, one commits the much worse error of reducing the love of God to the love of neighbor, rather than the other way around. In earlier times one sometimes reduced the love of neighbor to the love of God — though this identification occurred only on a very limited scale, among certain devout nuns rather than among significant theologians. In this identification one turns love of neighbor into a mere act of obedience toward Christ — one thinks that, if one is motivated by the love of Christ, it is enough to treat one's neighbor *as if* one loves him. But today's danger of reducing the love of God to the love of neighbor is incomparably worse and more dangerous, first because it is not limited to small groups but is found among theologians, in pastoral letters, and other places, and then secondly and especially because the direct love for Christ is far more important than love of neighbor, and because love of neighbor is possible for us only if we have the direct love for Christ, only if love of neighbor is objectively grounded in the love for Christ.

60. This horrible confusion, which overlooks all these essential differences, also manifests itself in the dreadful practice, especially in America, of replacing the pictures and statues of saints in the churches, and even of Jesus, with pictures of poor and suffering men.

17

Is Unity among the Faithful the Highest Value?

ONLY IF WE UNDERSTAND real love of neighbor and its holy
fire and power, as we find this in St. Paul, can we understand
that the anathema and excommunication are in no way opposed to the spirit of love of neighbor, but rather flow from
its true spirit. Of course, I am not here speaking of a condemnation by the Church which was followed by punishments
and execution that were imposed by the state, as was the
practice at the time of the Inquisition — these were of
course wrong and contrary to the spirit of love of neighbor.
I am rather speaking of the anathema as such and of that
excommunication which, first of all, solemnly and officially
condemns an heretical teaching, and secondly, excludes the
excommunicated person from the reception of the sacraments.
In the case of a priest it also necessarily suspends him, and
in the case of a theologian, removes him from his teaching

position. Such a condemnation is an act of love of God and of neighbor.

The anathema is an act of love of God because it condemns the offense against God which lies in the distortion of Christian revelation and of the teaching of the holy Church, and because it officially unmasks error as error. The protection of the divine Revelation has been entrusted to the holy Church, and to fulfil this holy trust is a central act of holy obedience and of love for divine truth, and indeed for God Himself. And it is an act of sublime love of neighbor to protect the faithful from the poison of false teachings, for it is a far more important and higher objective good for man to remain in the true faith, than to be relieved in his physical or psychic sufferings. The anathema is for men *in statu viae* (in their pilgrimage through life) something which protects that greatest good, which is so important for the salvation of their souls. It is thus a very great act of love because it protects the faithful from the deceits of heretics, who speak in the name of the Church, especially when they hold a position of authority and thus belong to the *ecclesia docens* (the teaching Church). These heretics are listened to with much sympathy and openness by the simple believing layman, and this makes it quite easy to seduce him to error and to poison his faith. Is it not a more fundamental, deeper act of love of neighbor to protect the faithful by unmasking heretics — and suspending them if they hold any office of authority — than to protect men against a plague, or to mitigate their poverty, or even to eliminate social injustice? Let us consider how seriously the anathema takes man as one who is called to eternal blessedness, as one who has the great dignity of belonging to the mystical body of Christ.

And even for him who is condemned it is an act of the

greatest love of neighbor. It is for him like the knife of a surgeon which cuts away the cancer of a patient. It is a fully earnest admonition, an enlightenment as to his errors, an invitation to return to the truth. It protects him from completely lapsing into heresy without fully realizing it — it enables him to grasp the full incompatibility of his theses with the teaching of the holy Church, to feel the significance of his error, and with terrible seriousness it forces him to decide "for or against God and His holy Church." If a spark of true faith in Christ and His holy Church still lives in him, he will turn away from the temptation which his heresy involves, and return to the community of the holy Church.

The vilification of the anathema — though it is through the anathema that the Church has preserved her identity and the purity of her teaching since St. Paul and throughout the centuries — is a typical consequence of distorting love of neighbor, and of confusing this love with a weak cheerfulness, niceness, and readiness to give in. The fear of the anathema betrays above all a loss of the *sensus supranaturalis,* a lapse into that this-worldliness which is more concerned with the earthly welfare of man than with his eternal salvation.

The distortion of love of neighbor is also expressed in the confusion of love of neighbor with community. I have already gone into this grave error in the Introduction to my book, *Celibacy and the Crisis of Faith.* I refer to it again here, not only because it is an especially disastrous error, but also because it is closely related to the vilification of the anathema and of excommunication.

Ecumenism Impossible toward Heretics in the Church

It must be said again with great emphasis that we can speak of ecumenism only with regard to religious communities which claim to be something completely different from the Catholic Church. First of all there is the Byzantine Orthodox Church, which is only schismatic. Secondly there are believing Protestants, who have for centuries not only been in schism, but have also formed a dogmatically distinct religious community. No Protestant would call himself Catholic, or claim to speak in the name of the holy Church. This holds even more for Jews, Moslems, Brahmans, or Buddhists. The attitude toward all these non-Catholics which Vatican II calls for under the name of ecumenism, can never be meaningfully directed to heretics within the Church.

The attitude which goes with true ecumenism (and it varies greatly according to the particular religion we are dealing with) involves sympathetically emphasizing the elements of truth in other religions while clearly rejecting the errors which they contain. But this attitude is never appropriate toward a Catholic who wants to remain in the Church and spread heresies and teachings contrary to those of the holy Church, and who often wants even to change the teaching of the Church. We should not keep any pseudo-community with these false teachers and destroyers of the Christian revelation and of Christian life in the holy Church. Full community is not even possible with those who are outside the Church and who have separated themselves from her. But the attitude which is right towards our separated brothers would be wrong towards heretics in the Church. Of course our love of neighbor must extend to these heretics. But even a certain loose community which is possible with our separated brothers (there are many degrees of this community, according to the different ones with whom we are dealing), is impossible with the heretics within the Church, because willy-nilly they are destroying the Church and poisoning her teaching, because they are abusing their apparent membership in her. Here we have to apply the words of St. John: "If someone comes to you and does not bring this doctrine, do not admit him into your house, or greet him. For whoever greets him, shares in his evil deeds" (2 John 10-11).

Truth and Community

There is another great danger which goes together with the distortion of love of neighbor: the danger of putting community above truth, and of implicitly making peace the highest value. Unfortunately this tendency to regard community as more important than truth is very widespread in the holy Church today.

The first great error which we find here is the separation of community from truth. All genuine community among men presupposes that they encounter one another in a certain realm of goods. The solidarity which comes from worshipping the same idol and working for it, or from working together for something false or evil, does not deserve the name of community. Such a pseudo-community is a definite evil, and possesses a disvalue. The value which community possesses as such is here poisoned by the disvalue of that which brings people together, of that in whose name they are united. Surely unity, community has a value of its own. The unity of man is something of value not only because it is the opposite of strife and struggle; it also has a value which is absent as long as individual men are indeed at peace, but not united in community. I have discussed the nature and value of community in my book, *Metaphysik der Gemeinschaft* (Metaphysics of Community). But what has to be especially emphasized today is that the formal nature and above all the value of community as such depend exclusively upon that "name" in which men are united. Community based upon error or something evil not only has no value, it has a definite disvalue. A pseudo-community built on some evil idol is something much worse than many individual, unrelated men who are in error or do evil. It is not only that it is worse for many to fall into error or heresy than for one to do so; it is not a question merely of a quantitative increase. No, it is the very unity of those who encounter one another in untruth and evil which gives birth to a pure disvalue and heightens the evil. The value of true community, the *concordia,* becomes in a pseudo-community a definite disvalue. Thus it is utterly impossible to separate community from truth, and to make community the most important thing. Community is dependent in both its nature and value on the truth on which it is built.

Secondly, in the religious sphere the thing of greatest value, that which glorifies God the most, is standing in the truth, possessing the true Faith. Christ has said: "Go into the world and teach all peoples. Whoever believes and is baptized will be saved, and whoever does not believe will be damned" (Mark 16: 15-16). The absolute importance which these words clearly ascribe to the true Faith, to faith in the true revelation of Christ, is in no way affected by the definition of Vatican I that God can give eternal blessedness to all men who lead a life in accord with the highest norms they know of.

The value of the truth and of the true Faith is thus undeniably greater than that of community, even if we are speaking of a genuine natural community built upon some real good. Indeed, the value of standing in the truth, and confessing the true God, is even greater than that of the marvelous community of the mystical body of Christ.

For it is in the true Faith and in real love of God that community with Him is constituted, and this is clearly the most important thing, and that from which all other community is dependent in its nature and value. The words of the Holy Thursday liturgy, *"congregavit nos in unum Christi amor"* (the love of Christ has brought us together and made us one), clearly express that it is only the love for Christ (which implies the true faith) which can establish this sublime unity among the faithful.

This overemphasis on community, on unity among men, this tendency to put unity above the truth and orthodoxy, is a consequence of the disastrous this-worldliness which is analogous to emphasizing love of neighbor at the expense of love of God. To hold that love of neighbor is the only manifestation of love of God and Christ, that they are both identical — one speaks hardly at all of the direct love for Christ, but makes up for this by speaking all the more of love of neighbor — is strictly analogous to placing community above orthodoxy.

18
The Cult of the "Positive"

::

WE HAVE ALREADY DISCUSSED the distortion of morality which follows from this-worldliness. Now we have to go into the following: with the catchword "positive" as opposed to "negative" the illusion is introduced that the avoidance of a sin is morally much less important than a purely positive moral deed. One criticizes the decalogue for containing too many prohibitions. One reproaches the Christian with overemphasizing the avoidance of evil and underemphasizing the doing of positive good. Thus today one constantly hears the demand for improving the world by fighting against poverty and for peace, but one hears little about overcoming our pride, about the struggle against temptations to impurity, the struggle against pharisaism, in a word, little about our own sanctification.

Here we have to distinguish between two different errors. First there is the this-worldly tendency to substitute work towards improving the world, for the sanctification of ourselves. Of this we have already spoken; it is the catastrophic tendency to concentrate our interest on improving the world instead of on glorifying God by our sanctification, and to fail to see the incomparable superiority of moral values over all merely morally relevant goods.

But is a second error which we want to deal with here — the foolishness involved in the catchword "positive." Let us consider first of all the superiority which a purely positive deed (such as giving alms) supposedly has over a deed which is considered negative such as resisting sin (of course negative here does not mean negative in value — any more than positive means positive in value). It is not the antithesis between good and evil which is at stake here, but rather that between positive deeds and omissions, the difference between yes and no.

One overlooks the fact that the conscious renunciation of sin is a fully positive act and possesses high moral values. Of course the mere objective absence of a sin — desirable as this is in itself — does not possess a moral value. We can be pleased that someone has not murdered another, but we cannot rightly consider him as possessing moral values as a result. If he never came into a situation in which he was tempted to kill another, then the fact that no sin, no great moral wrong was committed is indeed desirable, valuable, but it is only a pure absence of moral evil. With the absence of the murder there is of course also the absence of a great objective evil for the one who would have been the victim. But it is only a potential value which we find in the pure absence of a possible evil; there is no positive moral value in it. A person does not become endowed with moral values simply because he is not stained with some grave moral disvalue.

But the absence of a moral disvalue comes to possess a high moral value as soon as this absence is not just an objective fact but the result of a conscious renunciation of all moral evil, of a full "no" to the temptation to do moral wrong. The conscious rejection of all moral evil is inseparably bound up with a will directed to the morally good. Thus purity, which comes from a conscious rejection of everything impure, of every misuse of the sexual sphere, is a high positive virtue. We have to understand once and for all that a value response which rejects something, such as indignation, is just as positive as a value response which affirms some good.

The term positive loses all meaning as soon as one no longer looks at the object to which a given attitude refers. For, the kind of response we give, must and should accord with the kind of object which we are responding to. It is just as much required of us to reject error as to assent to truth. The rightness or adequacy of our response is determined by the nature of that to which we respond. If we prescind from the object to which it refers, a "yes" has no priority over a "no." Indignation over something evil is just as much a pure value response as enthusiasm for something good. Because both of these responses are fitting and appropriate with respect to their objects, and are indeed required by them, and because furthermore they both belong together, they both have a value, they are both something positive. As soon as one separates a "yes" or a "no" from the object to which it refers, and confers a value on the "yes" as such, then "positive" takes on a totally different meaning. When I said above that it loses all meaning when separated from the object, I intended to use the word "meaning" in the sense in which it can be applied to the relation between a response and its object.

Of course, in eternity there will no longer be any actualization of indignation because there will be no more moral evil, nor any suffering. But this absence of indignation in heaven does not come from the fact that indignation, being an act of rejection, is bad, but rather from the fact that there will be no more objects endowed with those disvalues which demand indignation. The infinite superiority of a situation in which there are no more evils and therefore nothing fit to be rejected by our response, must not be taken as proof that it is always better for us to say "Yes" than to say "No."

Furthermore, enthusiasm for the good is a source of happiness, whereas indignation over evil is not. The fact that some good with its objective value is realized is in itself a source of happiness and calls for the response of joy. The fact of an evil, especially of a moral evil, is in itself something infinitely sad, and demands the response of grief and pain. And apart from the joy in the one case and the pain in the other, the ability and "right" to be joyful is in itself a source of happiness, whereas the necessity and duty of being indignant is in itself a source of pain.

But this never justifies us in detaching "yes" and "no" from the objects to which they refer. And besides, the "no" to evil and error is potentially present in every "yes" to the good and the true.

Here we have to make an essential distinction between the rejection of evil when it confronts us as a temptation, and the rejection of it when we see it in other persons. Saying "no" to all sins which I could commit has a high moral value and is something thoroughly positive. Indignation over the sins of others is indeed also a response which is morally called for and is also thoroughly positive — but it does not have the same moral value. Saying "no" to temptation and sin is a central part of the moral life of man; so is hatred of sin in general. Indignation over the sins of others, over the offense which they give to God, belongs in a different category of morally positive attitudes and does not play the same central role which is played by the rejection of temptation.

Still another important distinction is the following: the rejection of sin in my own life is a pure act of my free will, whereas indignation over the offense given to God by others, as well as enthusiasm for their good deeds, is not in the same way subject to my will, even if it is not beyond all freedom. (Cf. Chapters 20-26 in my *Ethics,* which deal with freedom.)

But there are without a doubt types of persons who have a disposition to say, "no." There are men who feel better when they are rejecting evil in others. Their disposition is analogous to that of revolutionary types. They feel stronger and more independent as soon as they can protest; they would be unhappy if there were no opportunity to protest. It is as if they needed the existence of evils in order to come fully to themselves. They, of course, do not give a pure value response. It is a perversion to find it more satisfying to say, "no" than to say, "yes," to feel stronger in protest, revolution, in negating, to think that it is more serious and necessary to denounce evil than to affirm the good. These men also *see* evil much more than good; they often overlook everything that is good and desirable, and even morally edifying, but they see clearly everything that is wrong.

Now this disposition involves a regrettable and unfortunate lack of objectivity. But the opposite disposition is just as wrong: men who are so harmless and unsuspecting that they overlook evil and who are enthusiastic without reason, are also unobjective. Even if this attitude is more agreeable than the one which sees evil everywhere and is full of mistrust (just as the optimist is more agreeable than the pessimist), it is nevertheless morally just as defective. It involves a disvalue because of its lack of objectivity and blindness, and it does not have ultimate moral earnestness. This "positivity" is no value at all.

But let us now consider the type to which we are referring in this chapter, the one who is not at all objective, who separates himself from the nature of the objects of his responses, and who approaches the world in an attitude which he has assumed long before approaching it. Here we enter the realm of prejudices, the realm where we speak of optimists and pessimists, where a purely subjective temperamental disposition modifies our relation to the world and replaces those meaningful responses which are dictated by the objects of our responses. This lack of objectivity is a disvalue. The optimist is perhaps a more agreeable person than the pessimist, but they are both caught up in a lack of objectivity which is a disvalue.

This lack of objectivity is much worse in the case of the man who is by temperament constantly annoyed without reason and who inclines to complain about everything. But the disvalue which lies in the unobjectivity of annoyance — and as distinguished from anger, annoyance is never a value response but always contains an unobjective element of subjective irritation — does not prove that it is always a mistake to say, "no," and does not prove that there is something wrong with the meaningful and required value response of indignation.

Let us just mention still another way of rejecting evil which must not be confused with a value-responding rejection such as indignation. There is a pharisaical way of preferring to reject evil rather than to affirm the good. Sometimes such a person enjoys his superiority by dwelling on the mistakes of others, sometimes he regards himself as morally outstanding by energetically condemning evil. All pharisaical self-enjoyment is incompatible with the spirit of true value response and is morally damnable. It possesses a great moral disvalue. But this disvalue is not found in every gesture of rejection, it is not found in that indignation which is appropriate to and called for by some immorality, but only in pharisaical self-enjoyment — that should be immediately clear to anyone.

And so we have to emphasize again: the rejection of evil and of sin is a response which is purely positive and morally called for, and it possesses a high moral value. One cannot truly love God, without hating the devil. One cannot really love the truth, without hating error. One cannot find the truth and grasp it clearly as such, without seeing through errors. Knowledge of truth is inseparably linked with knowledge of error, with the unmasking of error.[61] All talk about the superiority of "yes" over "no," about the "negativity" of rejecting that which should be rejected, is so much idle chatter.

In earlier times there were of course moral theologians who overemphasized the avoidance of sin and who underemphasized performing morally good deeds. Especially with regard to the whole sexual sphere, they spoke much of the disvalue of misuse, and often warned against sexual sins, but neglected to unfold the values of right use. One did not speak of the mystery of this sphere, of the mysterious union and self-donation in the consummation of marriage, of the great beauty of this "becoming one flesh," which is an organic expression of spousal love and a fulfilment of the desire for union with the beloved (of this union our Lord said, "And the two shall become one flesh") which is rooted in spousal love. One emphasized onesidedly the disvalue of misusing sex because one failed to see the great value of this God-given fulfilment of spousal love and the great value of this mutual self-donation in marriage. Not until the wonderful allocutions of Pope Pius XII was this positive aspect of the sexual sphere fully recognized, not until then was the value of the bodily union in marriage and its relation to spousal love, proclaimed by the highest Church authority.[62]

But in the entire literature of the great theologians — St. Augustine, St. Thomas, Duns Scotus, St. Francis de Sales, Moehler, Scheeben, Gratry, Newman — we find no emphasis on the avoidance of sin at the expense of good actions and attitudes.

Here we come across an important point in the nonsense surrounding the catchword "positive." One forgets that there is a hierarchy in our duties toward God: our first duty is not to offend God by sin; our second is to glorify Him by good deeds. We can express this philosophically by saying that our first moral task is not to introduce morally relevant evils into the world, and not to destroy morally relevant goods — for instance, not to torture or kill a man, not to commit injustice, consciously to spread error, or work for apostasy. Our second task is the mitigation or elimination of those morally relevant evils which we find — for instance, relieving the suffering of our neighbor, helping a sick person, fighting injustice, freeing those who are unjustly imprisoned, and above all, helping someone to find his way to God, helping him to convert to the holy Church. Only in coming to man's third moral task do we come to the producing of morally relevant goods — for instance, providing some happiness for another person, helping a gifted person to complete his studies, doing good for one's neighbor in different ways.[63]

This hierarchy has a definite character. It is not a hierarchical order which says that what comes first has a greater value than what comes second and third. It is rather a hierarchy which refers to our tasks, our mission. What is the first thing which is morally demanded of us, or as we could ask, "What is the minimum?" The answer to this question is not necessarily that which is most important.

Avoiding moral evil — and we commit evil in producing morally relevant evils or in destroying morally relevant goods — although it is something negative, has priority over the realization of morally relevant good, which is something positive. This priority of the negative over the positive is an objective fact and has nothing to do with the negative attitude of moral pessimism, nothing to do with an overemphasis on disvalues. It is no sign of a negative attitude to emphasize the priority of avoiding sin. We avoid offending God by sin when we abstain from bringing into being morally relevant evils, as well as from rebellion against God and all negative attitudes which make a direct gesture of defiance against God, such as cursing, indifference to God, etc. This omission of what is morally bad and of sin is an eminent expression of obedience and love of God — it is a definite value response. It is a total misunderstanding to call this omission negative in comparison with bringing morally relevant goods into being, or with actively relieving the need of another or working to improve the world.

There are of course sins which come from neglecting to do some good thing. These play a great role in the Gospel, as when Christ says, "I was thirsty and you did not give me to drink, naked and you did not cloth me" (Mt. 25:35). These belong in the class of our second moral task, the mitigation of the evils which exist. But is is deeply meaningful that in the ten commandments the negative ones, the prohibitions — the second, fifth, sixth, seventh, and eighth — play such a great role; and that Christ, too, gives us prohibitions when he condemns pharisaism, pride, detraction. The tendency today to speak little of avoiding sin and to emphasize doing good — all under the slogan, "We want to be positive" — is a clear distortion of the moral sphere, it is at bottom a utilitarian lack of interest in moral values as distinguished from morally relevant values. These are so many symptoms and consequences of the disastrous this-worldliness.

Natural and Worldly Goods

We mentioned above that there is a certain disposition which sees everything negative more clearly, and then the opposite disposition which sees everything positive first of all and more clearly, and we also discussed the lack of objectivity in the pessimist and the optimist. Now we want to emphasize how important it is from a religious point of view to see objectively the whole situation of our earthly life and of the world as far as we know it, that is, to see objectively the two really existing aspects of the world. Here we see how wonderfully the holy Church has expressed the existence of both aspects in her liturgy. Earth is called a "vale of tears," and yet it says in the Gloria, "heaven and earth are full of your glory." Even earth contains great goods which proclaim the goodness, glory, and beauty of God.

In the phrase, "vale of tears," the tragedy of human life is fully recognized, especially the fearfulness of death, the disharmony which was brought into the world by the fall and which continues even after our redemption by Christ, the tragedy of the temporary triumph of evil, all the unhappy

marriages, all children who have gone astray, all disappoint-
ments — and most of all, as the greatest human cross, the
death of beloved persons. On the other hand, when it says,
"heaven *and earth* are full of your glory," the magnificence
of creation is recognized, the beauty of nature, which speaks
to us of the infinite glory of God, the deep happiness which
is conferred on us by the beauty of nature and of all great
art, the unspeakable glory of a great human love! What an
invention of God is marriage! How marvelous that there
exists such a fulfilment of spousal love, that such a union
between persons is possible! What a great gift of God it is
that, as the beautiful Fulda Ritual says, the coming into being
of new human beings is entrusted to the sweet love between
man and woman. And what a gift is the ability to know; here
I speak not only of the general ability to know which belongs
to the nature of the person, but also of the ability to attain
systematic knowledge, and especially true philosophical
knowledge. Of this Socrates says in the *Apology* (no. 41),
referring to his condition after death: "But then I will be
able to continue my investigation of true knowledge and of
pseudo-knowledge; and just as in this world I have tried to
find out who is wise and who only says that he is without
really being so, so I will continue this investigation in the
next world." Indeed, what a gift is being itself, our existence
as persons, as well as what Goethe calls "des Lebens holde
Gewohnheit." We cannot continue here going through the
magnificence of creation, the riches of all great natural goods
(which are different from merely "worldly goods.") Let us
just refer to some of the saints and holy men in the Church
who have sung the praises of the message of God to be found
even in the natural creation: St. Augustine, St. Anselm, St.

Francis of Assisi, St. Bonaventure, St. Thomas Aquinas, Cardinal Newman, Pope Pius XII.

But in order fully to understand and duly to appreciate the great natural goods, we have to understand the following. First, we have to distinguish these real natural goods from merely worldly goods, such as wealth, power, fame, influence. All these are only *utenda* (things to be used), never *fruenda* (things to be rested in and enjoyed). Here I can only refer to my detailed discussion of this in my book, *The Sacred Heart*. Worldly goods are by no means bad in themselves, but they contain great danger; they are to be used as means to something else, to be used in order to do good, to bring things of value into being, but not to be aimed at for their own sake and to be enjoyed.

Secondly, real natural goods show their ultimate value only in Christ, that is, only when their message from God and His infinite glory is understood, as for instance St. Francis of Assisi understood the beauty of nature. Natural goods are really understood only when we see how they point beyond themselves to something infinitely higher and seem to say to us, as St. Augustine puts it, "We are not the source of ultimate happiness." It is a great mystery that they show us their innermost depth, their ultimate value, only when we do not regard them as the highest good, when we do not take them just in themselves, separate from everything else, but see them in the light of infinitely superior supernatural goods, in the light of the infinite beauty and holiness of Christ.

Thirdly, everything gets its true background, its ultimate proportions, from the revelation of Christ, from knowing the meaning of our life, knowing that life is a *status viae* (state of pilgrimage), knowing the truth of the "promise" which lies in all great natural goods. For all these goods point beyond themselves and contain as it were the "promise" that there must be an eternal life, an absolute world, of which they are just messengers. If there were no life after death, no eternal blessedness, then all these great earthly goods would be merely a façade, an illusion, they would promise something which does not exist.

Plato had a deep intimation of this. But it is not until the revelation of Christ that we learn of the full reality of that which the natural goods somehow promise. Only the revelation of Christ triumphs over the deep tragedy which surrounds these goods because of death and because of their transitoriness. And, above all, the redemption of Christ opens for us the way to a world of glory which does not pass away, a world where God wipes away all tears.

The revelation of Christ has not only disclosed to us the world of supernatural glory, the world of holiness, which infinitely surpasses the beauty of all the greatest natural goods. Our redemption through Christ's death on the cross, and the communication to us of a supernatural principle of life in baptism, has opened for us the way to eternal blessedness, and has given us hope of it. This radically changes the nature of the "vale of tears." Of course in one sense the seriousness of life and the tragedy of the "vale of tears" is heightened by our knowing of the true situation of man, by knowing of the alternative of eternal blessedness or eternal punishment in hell. In addition to all natural suffering there is added for the believer the holy fear of eternal damnation; as we say in the *Dies Irae, "quod sum miser tunc dicturus, quem patronum rogaturus cum vix justus sit securus"* ("O what will I then say in my wretchedness? What protector will I call to my defense, when even the just are hardly safe?"). But still, our whole life *in statu viae* (on pilgrimage), in this "vale of tears," is filled with light because of our hope of the beatific vision for all eternity, our hope for an indestructible communion of love face to face with Christ.

The primacy of joy over all suffering is revealed to us in Christ, and thus the joyful aspect of creation, as distinguished from its "vale of tears" aspect, necessarily presupposes the primacy of supernatural goods over all natural goods, even the highest ones. As soon as the absolute primacy of supernatural goods is no longer seen, and the glorification of God through our sanctification no longer concerns us more than all natural goods, then we become blind to the true value of natural goods and to the happiness which they give, we lose a sense of their hierarchy, and even of the difference between worldly and natural goods. Thus the shift of stress to this world in no way involves a deeper appreciation of real natural goods. The "positive" attitude toward the world which goes with this-worldliness, is in reality, although some are so proud of it, that unjustified optimism which Bernanos rightly called "a substitute for hope designed for idiots and cowards." This "positive" attitude comes only from forgetting the words of Christ, "What does it profit a man to gain the whole world, and suffer the loss of his soul" (Mt. 16:26).

Let us summarize: First: the chatter about the priority of the "positive" — the slogan, "We must approach positively the tendencies of our time"; "It is better to affirm than to deny"; "The anathema and excommunication are too negative" — is a foolish and dangerous error. For to reject what is false and untrue is just as positive as to affirm what is true. To reject what is evil is just as positive as to affirm what is good — and besides, both are inseparably linked. The affirmation of truth and the love of what is good is implicitly contained in every rejection of untruth or evil which is objectively justified, and vice versa.

Secondly, every "positive" action and attitude which is not meaningfully directed to some object, is just as bad a prejudice as a "negative" action or attitude which is not meaningfully directed to some object.

Thirdly, one can understand that the world is full of the glory of God only in understanding that it is a "vale of tears." As soon as one is denied at the expense of the other, both the positive and the negative are distorted.

Fourthly, true understanding for natural goods is so linked with the absolute primacy of supernatural goods that the shift of emphasis to this world does not deepen our grasp of the value of natural goods, but renders it mediocre. Although we supposedly leave our ghetto by primarily emphasizing the improvement of the world, this is in reality no "positive" attitude but rather a loss of true positivity. We attain to true positivity only in directing our glance to eternity, only in being concerned with the glorification of God through our sanctification, only in leading a life that is permeated by the realization that we are redeemed by Christ and have hope of seeing Him in the beatific vision: "Seek first the kingdom of God, and all these things will be added to you."

The true mission of the Church is not to improve the face of the world but to glorify God by the sanctification of men, and to secure their salvation. To shift the emphasis from eternity to the future, to devote all our energies to a happier earthly future for mankind, for progress toward a better world, to mobilize men for this ideal — to neglect the glorification of God, the sanctification of the individual, and his eternal blessedness — would not only deprive the Church of her *raison d'etre* (reason for being), but would condemn mankind "to sit in the shadow of death."

In order to see clearly the use of positive and negative as slogans, let us, in conclusion distinguish this from another and legitimate use of these terms. In the history of the Church there have been two different attitudes toward great natural goods: the one has been called the positive way, the other the negative. In his book, Abbot Butler has referred to these two ways in the Church.

According to the negative way, total abandonment to Christ necessarily involves a turning away from all natural goods. One should love only God for His own sake, all natural goods are only means for this. Only God is a true object of *frui* (resting in and enjoying), all other things are only objects of *uti* (using). This was the view of St. Augustine right after his conversion at the time of his *Soliloquies*. But later he changed his attitude toward natural goods and required only that one love them all in God, and love God infinitely more than them; as he said: "Husband, love your wife, and wife, love your husband — but love Christ still more." [64]

We find this "negative" attitude to natural goods in Dionysius the Areopagite, in the *Imitation of Christ* by Thomas a Kempis, in St. John of the Cross; we find the "positive" attitude in the later works of St. Augustine, in St. Bonaventure, St. Catherine of Siena, St. Francis de Sales, and Cardinal Newman. Both attitudes have been recognized in the Church as completely compatible with the Christian Revelation. I must admit that in all my works I have defended the "positive" attitude to natural goods by showing the mission which natural goods have to lead us to God, and by emphasizing the possibility and value of *amare in Deo* (loving them in God).

But the terms "positive" and "negative" have here a totally different meaning from their meaning as slogans; and both the positive way and the negative way in the Church are equally and radically opposed to that shift of emphasis to this world which is praised as "positive." For we find the absolute primacy of supernatural goods in both of the two classical ways. In neither one of them is there any shift of emphasis to this world. In the representatives of the positive way we find concern with glorifying God, with *commerce intime* with Jesus. Both ways are directed to eternity and not to an earthly future, in both there is the same passionate love for holiness, the same striving for sanctification, in both contemplation plays a great role next to action, in both our first moral task is seen to be the avoidance of offending God by sin. So we see that "positive" and "negative," as designations of two different attitudes towards great natural goods, have nothing to do with the use of these terms in the slogan: "Let us above all be positive, let us concern ourselves less with the condemnation of heresies and with opposition to sin, and more with the improvement of social conditions in the world."

NOTES

61. Thus Cardinal Newman says in his *Grammar of Assent*: "I would maintain that fear of error is simply necessary to the genuine love of truth."

62. Cf. my book, *In Defense of Purity: An Analysis of the Catholic Ideals of Purity and Virginity* (Chicago: Franciscan Herald Press, 1970).

63. Thus St. Augustine, in his *City of God*, XIX, 14: "This moral order imposes on man, first the duty not to harm anyone, and then, secondly, the duty to be of help to everyone where possible."

64. Cf. Dr. Alice Jourdain, *Uti and Frui* (Master's Dissertation, Fordham University, 1946).

19

The Eruption of Collectivism in the Holy Church

:::

WE WANT TO TURN NOW to another unfortunate error which goes together with the shift of emphasis to this world and to the humanitarian improvement of it, and which especially goes together with the replacing of eternity with an earthly future. I mean collectivism, and the tendency to neglect the individual person with the slogan that we live in a time in which a sense of community has awakened and in which the "collectivist" features of the Church must be emphasized. (This is the position of Fr. Lombardi in his book, *Towards a Better World*.) This collectivist tendency comes out especially in the new missal.

One imagines that this tendency represents real progress, a real breakthrough, an overcoming of religious egoism and "devotionalism." But this is unfortunately a great illusion. As I mentioned before, one fails to understand that it is not only an error to emphasize community at the expense of the dignity and value of the individual person, but that this never leads to true community, but rather to a collective. One forgets that the person ranks higher than any natural community, as Max Scheler rightly insisted. Although the state and the nation have a longer life than the individual man, only man has an immortal soul, only he transcends earthly existence — states and nations, when they die, simply cease to be. In addition to this, the person is what in metaphysics we call a full substance, whereas natural communities are not. The difference between personal and non-personal being is the greatest of all ontological differences except for the difference between finite and infinite being, as we have already stated.

The superiority of the individual person over all natural communities is strikingly stated by Kierkegaard in his discussion of the superiority of the individual over the species in his work, *Point of View for My Work as an Author*: "Mankind differs from an animal race not merely by its general superiority as a race, but by the *human* characteristic that every single individual within the race (not merely distinguished individuals but every individual) is more than the race." And in his *Journals* he writes: "In the animal world 'the individual' is always less important than the race. But it is the peculiarity of the human race that just because the individual is created in the image of God 'the individual' is above the race."

Now let us make the distinction within community between the I-Thou community, and the we-community. I have developed this distinction in my book, *Metaphysik der Gemeinschaft* (Metaphysics of Community). In all human relations these two dimensions are actualized according to the situation. But certain relations are on the whole primarily I-Thou communities, as in marriage, whereas in the relation between brother and sister, it is primarily a we-community which is at stake.[65]

In the I-Thou relation the two persons face one another; for each the other is a Thou. In the we-relation persons stand as it were next to one another, and hand in hand they face some good, the truth, some other person.

Now from this difference we have to separate another one which is very important for our context. I mean the difference between the community which builds on an I-Thou relation, that is, on any kind of love, and that community with many other men whom we do not know individually. This is what we find in the case of a state or of a nation. Here men are parts of the communal body, and their relation with one another is established by the relation of the individual to the whole, that is, it is a result of the relation of part to whole as found between the individual and the communal body.

The human person is destined for both kinds of community, for both the I-Thou community as well as for life in a communal body. The person has the ability to build up a communal body with others. We cannot really understand the nature of the person without understanding that it is capable of both kinds of community and ordered to both. As I showed in my *Metaphysik der Gemeinschaft,* the human person is on the one hand "a world in itself" as no other contingent being is, and is on the other hand capable of a relation to other persons which completely surpasses all forms of union in the nonpersonal world, such as the fusion of several material substances into one substance. For these reasons it is completely false ever to try to put the community above the individual person, to emphasize community at the expense of the individual person. But the failure to understand the dignity and value of the person is not only one of the gravest of errors, as already stated, but it also undermines from the very beginning the nature of true community, and replaces the community with the collective. The person can never be understood apart from its ability to enter into both kinds of community, and of its being ordered to both.

Person and community are so ordered to one another that we understand the dignity and value of true community only in understanding the unique dignity of the person, and the new world of being which dawns in the person. The full understanding for the nature and value of community presupposes the ontological superiority of the person over all natural communities. On the other hand, it belongs to the nature of the human person that it is made for community — and only persons are capable of community.

Now if we apply this to our subject we understand that real transcendence and the conquest of egoism lies only in self-donation to a Thou, and not in the consciousness of being part of a greater whole.

True transcendence and the real conquest of egoism comes primarily from our abandonment to God: as St. Augustine says, "You have made us, O Lord, for Yourself." This is that I-Thou relation for which the person was primarily created. This turning to God suffices to break through all immanentism, all imprisonment in ourselves, all egoism. This is, as we will see, true expansiveness. Only in this I-Thou abandonment can we be liberated from the ghetto of our self-centeredness and narrowness. Only in this liberation do we attain at the same time to the full unfolding of our true self — this is in sharp distinction to today's fashionable "self-fulfilment," which is only self-imprisonment in the ghetto of our selfishness. As Christ says, "Whoever loses his life for my sake, will find it" (Mt. 10: 39).

Of course, in love of neighbor (which, as we saw, is rooted in love for Christ and presupposes this love) there is also a real transcendence, a real conquest of egoism. But love of neighbor is directed to a thou, to an individual person, even though any man can become my neighbor in a given situation. Indeed, there is a transcendence in all the kinds of love, whether love of parents or of children, whether friendship or spousal love, although the transcendence here differs from that which we find in love of neighbor and love of God.[66]

But in feeling ourselves to be parts of a whole, members of a natural community, there is, in sharp distinction to self-donation to an individual thou, neither any real transcendence nor any real conquest of egoism. This is why Dostoevsky says that love for mankind is usually only self-love (as distinguished from love of neighbor). The consciousness of being a part of something much greater, of something which I feel to be much more important than I am and my personal life is, neither liberates me from egoism, nor enables me to find myself in the God-given way.

This "feeling small" with respect to the whole — in pantheism one is led to feel that one is only a speck of dust in the universe — leads easily to a false loss of oneself and to a depersonalization; and the idea of being a part of a great whole easily leads at the same time to the satisfaction of pride. In *The Trojan Horse,* and earlier in my *Transformation in Christ* (Ch. 7), I have discussed this way of satisfying pride. Von Kuehnelt-Leddhin wittily calls this attitude "nostrism." We encounter it in nationalism, where people say, "I am nothing, but the country to which I belong is the most important and outstanding in the world." Similarly, in "epochalism" people say, "Of course, I am nothing special; but I live in an era which is superior to all earlier ones." Such people regard their time as the most progressive, and as culturally and morally superior to all earlier times, and they look down upon these earlier times with contempt. The mere fact of living in the modern period and of moving with the *Zeitgeist* (spirit of the times) satisfies their pride. We find something analogous in trying to break the bonds of our self-imprisonment, not by self-donation to a Thou, but by feeling ourselves to be parts of a communal body. Here we are concerned with confusing the depersonalization of collectivism with a liberating transcendence, with getting out of the ghetto of our egoism. In reality this loss of interest in the individual, in favor of the community, is a lapse into depersonalization, into the destruction of true community, which is thereby reduced to a collective.

Collectivism and depersonalization are specific characteristics of our era. Many persons fail to understand that these features of today's world are prevailing more and more. Such persons even praise this collectivism by calling it something "global," or they interpret it as a "coming closer to God" which is occurring independently of our freedom.

There is no need to speak of the collectivism in Communism. But the collectivistic tendency is not limited to Communist countries; it is present in a different form in those countries which are especially proud of their democratic constitutions and which constantly speak of democracy. As we saw in Chapter 4, the state with its laws is more and more interfering with the sacred human rights of the individual, with his intimate personal life. In America teachers are forbidden, under the slogan of "separation of Church and State," to speak of God in school — although at the same time a world view of atheism and amoralism is inflicted on the students. But this depersonalization, this disrespect of the individual person, this brain-washing is not limited to America. With few exceptions it is being spread everywhere today by the so highly celebrated mass media of radio and television. I have already spoken at length about this point. It is enough in our present context again to call attention to the collectivistic and depersonalizing tendency which prevails in our time.

Until now it was always one of the glorious tasks of the holy Church to work in a special way against the dangerous tendencies which as it were fill the air of an era and take on a certain historical-sociological actuality. In the age of rationalism the Church emphasized the limits of reason, in the age of romanticism she emphasized the importance and mission of reason, in the age of liberalism the magnificent Syllabus of Pius IX unmasked the dangers of liberalism. The danger of collectivism, of idolizing the state, of depersonalization was opposed in the various condemnations of Communism and in the wonderful encyclical *Mit brennender Sorge*.[67] But today one constantly hears: "The Church must go with the times, *aggiornamento* is necessary if she is to keep her life, indeed, if she is to keep on in existence at all." One links the slogan of "adapting to the times" with the slogan of "abandoning the ghetto." One forgets the words of him who coined the concept of *aggiornamento,* Pope John XXIII: the Church must imprint her image on the various countries and eras, and not the other way around.

There is no doubt but that depersonalization and collectivism go hand in hand with the shift of emphasis from the next world to this world, from sanctifying the individual to improving the face of the world, from eternity to the earthly future. As soon as the glorification of God and the eternal blessedness of souls, take second place to progress and to the improvement of the world, then the ultimate seriousness of the fate of every individual soul is no longer understood, the incomparable superiority of the individual person over all natural communities is no longer recognized. Hence the words of Cardinal Newman:

"The Church regards this world, and all that is in it, as a mere shadow, as dust and ashes, compared with the value of one single soul. She holds that, unless she can, in her own way, do good to souls, it is no use her doing anything. . . . She considers the action of this world and the action of the soul simply incommensurate, viewed in their respective spheres; she would rather save the soul of one single wild bandit of Calabria, or a whining beggar of Palermo, than draw a hundred lines of railroad through the length and breadth of Italy, or carry out a sanitary reform, in its fullest details, in every city of Sicily, except so far as these great national works tended to some spiritual good beyond them."[68]

As soon as one no longer sees that an immortal soul is incomparably more important than all social improvement and progress of civilization, one has fallen victim to collectivism and depersonalization.

One needs only to think of the unfortunate dialogues with Communists in which Catholics try to find a common ground by the equivocal use of the term "future"; here the primacy of the individual soul is completely given up.

But this collectivistic tendency is found even in the friendly attitude toward the Communists, in the illusion of winning them over and even converting them to Catholicism by approaching them in patience. Instead of opposing the catastrophic danger of collectivism, one sees it as a sign of the times which one thinks calls for accommodation.

One forgets that Christ always addressed only individual souls; as Kierkegaard emphasizes in his *Purity of Heart*: God knows only the individual and not the mass.

Sacred community among Christians can only grow out of the love for Christ, as we saw above. This sacred community must "pass through" the intimate personal union with Christ. The words of Christ, "Where two or three are gathered together in my name, there I am in the midst of them" (Mt. 18:20), are often wrongly interpreted. One thinks that community as such draws Christ into our midst. One forgets the decisive importance of the words, "in my name." These words, which Christ also uses in speaking of that prayer to God which will be heard, include many things and refer to a basis of Christian community which goes beyond merely aiming at community.

They include full faith in Christ, a deep bond of love with Christ as He is encountered in every individual, meeting other Christians in Christ — here the individual soul goes beyond its union with Jesus and attains to a holy union with others which is possible only in and through Him. We see how deep is the union with Christ which is meant by the words "in my name," when we consider His words, "Until now you have not asked the Father anything in my name." Prayer to God becomes something totally new through the "name of Jesus," it takes on a completely new quality. It is not just that Christ intercedes for us, as does our Lady or a saint, thus giving our petition more weight in the eyes of God. "Prayer in His name" is prayer in Jesus, in His spirit, in deep supernatural union with Him.

On the other hand, the tremendous value which Christ ascribes to that community which is rooted in Him, is revealed in the words, "Where two or three are gathered together in my name. . . ." That He is present when men gather in His name shows the whole importance of this holy community.

The important thing for us is to distinguish this unique holy community with others, from all natural communities in which one gathers together in the name of some ideal, or some practical goal. When we fall into this-worldliness, collectivism, and when we do not clearly distinguish between the sacred and the profane, then we become blind to the unique character of the sacred community in Christ, and to the immense difference between this community and purely natural communities.

We will understand this better if we briefly consider the different forms which the presence of Christ can take. The first is that presence of Christ in our soul of which St. Paul says, "Not I live, but Christ lives in me" (Gal. 2:20). It is that presence of Christ which comes when He builds up His kingdom in a soul, when He says, "He is in me and I am in Him" (Jn. 6:56).

From this centrally important presence in the individual soul, which of course presupposes the pouring out of a supernatural principle of life in baptism, we have to distinguish the presence of Christ in the midst of those who are gathered in His name. This is a new kind of presence, which however presupposes the first.

Here we are speaking only of the various kinds of presence of Christ, and not of the ways of being united with Him. We are of course in an eminent way united with Him by being a member of His Mystical Body. This union with Christ is inseparably linked with the new supernatural principle of life which is received in baptism.

A completely new kind of presence of Christ is His presence on the altar. The great miracle of consecration at Mass lies of course in the transformation of bread into the real living, glorified Body of Christ, and of wine into His real Blood united with His Body. This bodily presence of Christ in the consecrated Host is something utterly different from His presence in the midst of those who are gathered together in His name.[69]

From this bodily presence in the holy sacrifice of the Mass, we have to distinguish the completely different presence of Christ in the soul of him who receives Holy Communion. This mysterious union comes from the fact that the individual receives as food the real Body of Christ.

Against the background of this brief discussion of the different kinds of the presence of Christ, we want now to deal with the danger of emphasizing the collective.

In emphasizing the meal rather than the unbloody re-enactment of the sacrifice of Calvary, rather than His becoming really present in the Mass, community with the other faithful is made the main thing. The main theme of the holy Mass — the re-enactment of the sacrifice of Calvary, by which God is unspeakably glorified — is thrust into the background. One forgets that the glorification of God is the center of the holy Mass, and that each individual, together with all the other faithful, has the privilege of participating in this glorification which the priest as representative of Christ carries out. The earlier practice of the priest facing the altar was a deep expression of this: the faithful looked with the priest toward the altar, and they were drawn by him into the mystery of the sacrifice. This was a deep Christ-centered gesture: the priest, who represents Christ, was shown to be that mediator at Mass whom we follow — and he was himself completely directed to God.

At Communion comes the unique and mysterious union

of the individual soul with Jesus. This is a new theme organically linked with the main theme of the Mass. First there is the complete turning to the Father, ultimate abandonment to Him; then Christ's love overflows and He comes to each individual soul, He enters into each individual soul and feeds it with His bodily presence, and at the same time He takes the individual soul into Himself. Through this union of Christ with the individual soul, there comes into being a bond of union with all those who receive His holy Body. It is an incomprehensible mystery: Christ remains one and the same, it is the same Body which we all receive, it is undivided — and through it a unity with the other faithful is established which goes far beyond that unity which comes from gathering in His name.

But as soon as one makes the shared meal the main thing, one is trying to skip over that which is incomparably more important. In this way even the sacred community, the supernatural meal, is distorted. Here we have a specific infection of collectivism, an emphasis on community at the expense of the individual person. The result is that one loses precisely that which one wants to attain. For this holy community with others — or at least the consciousness of community — at the sacred meal, a community which is radically different from all natural communities, can never be achieved when the true hierarchy of things is upset. This is the true sacred hierarchy: first the glorification of God, where we are directed exclusively to God in adoration, then the intimate union of love with Jesus in Holy Communion, and finally the triumphant unity with all the faithful who are present, as well as with the entire Church. As soon as one aims at this unity directly and ignores this sacred hierarchy, one loses the unity and replaces it, at least subjectively, with a profane unity, such as we might find in an association of army veterans. Blindness to the sacred as well as secularization go hand in hand with an overemphasis on the "collective," with the triumph of collectivism.

NOTES

65. Cf. the Introduction to my *Celibacy and the Crisis of Faith,* pp. xxix-xxxiv.

66. My book *Das Wesen der Liebe* has dealt with the various forms of transcendence.

67. See note 57.

68. Newman, *Difficulties of Anglicans,* vol. II, part II, lecture 8, par. 4.

69. Henri de Lubac, in his book, *Le Surnaturel,* reports that this presence, which today we call the mystical presence, was in the earliest age of the Church called the real presence, and the presence of Christ in the consecrated Host was called the mystical presence. This changes nothing with regard to the radical difference of the two kinds of presence. The later terminology, which is also that of Trent, is in any case much more adequate, because it is appropriate to call a bodily presence by the name of Real Presence.

20

Democratization of the Holy Church

AFTER DEALING WITH the terrible danger of being infected by collectivism, a danger which is a logical consequence of the shift of emphasis from eternity to this world, we want now to deal briefly with another disastrous consequence of this shift of emphasis: the "democratization" of the Church.

Here, too, as with collectivism, we sense the thoroughly mediocre atmosphere of today's world, instead of that holy light which comes from above and transfigures this world. And to radiate this light is one of the glorious characteristics of the holy Church. It is her task to confront in the light of Christ all those new problems which emerge from various situations. She must ever and again let us hear the voice of Christ and she should never adapt herself to the spirit of the times. For we should never forget that if the Church is *in* this world, she is not *of* this world. In spite of all the imperfections of her members she bears witness even in her external structure that she is of divine origin.[70]

The Church is not only the bride of Christ, but also the mother of the saints. Through all the changes of history she has kept her identity as the one who proclaims and protects the revelation of Christ. What we want to show here is that, if we are not intoxicated by the holy radiance of the Church, if this does not awaken us to a burning love for her, then we can no longer understand that laws hold for her that are different from those which would hold even in a perfect world, and that what is good and useful in a natural sphere is not necessarily applicable to her.

Democracy, rightly understood, is undoubtedly something good for the state. The primary value of democracy lies in its respect for the inalienable human rights of the individual person, in its radical opposition to any kind of totalitarian interference by the state with those rights which man has directly received from God and which concern the shape of his private life. The totalitarian conception of the state is linked to the idea that the individual person exists primarily for the state, that the state surpasses in value the individual person. But true democracy starts with the dignity of the individual person, and sharply opposes the view of man as a mere means for the state. Communism, and earlier Nazism, embody the full totalitarian antithesis to any true democracy. In Mussolini's Fascism we find in a mild form, and not so consistently carried out, the thesis of Hegel that the state is a higher reality than the individual person, that the human person is primarily to be considered as a member of the state, that the value of the person depends on what it can accomplish for the state. Needless to say, anything colored with totalitarianism goes hand in hand with collectivism. Democracy rightly understood, which does not refer primarily to the political form of a state but to the right relation of the state to the individual person, is opposed to any collectivism, and recognizes the fact that the person is by no means mainly a member of the state and by no means exhausts his being in belonging to the state.

Although this anti-totalitarian feature of democracy is its first and most important feature, democracy also involves a participation of all citizens in the government of the republic. It not only affirms sacred human rights of the person, it also grants the person certain political rights. Maritain has written much on this and on the value of this aspect of democracy. In this respect democracy also represents an antithesis to an authoritarian state. But the antithesis to totalitarianism is of course much more important — this is the greatest value of democracy. Totalitarianism is a horrible error, a monstrosity in the eyes of God, and utterly incompatible with the Christian revelation. Democracy as an antithesis to an authoritarian state may be better and, unless extraordinary situations temporarily require an authoritarian structure, more pleasing to God. But all authoritarian governments, such as the monarchies of earlier times or certain oligarchies, as in Venice, cannot as such be called a monstrosity in the eyes of God, nor can they even be called incompatible with the Gospel. Only a prejudiced man can regard as purely negative the state of St. Louis, king of France, which did not contain any trace of totalitarianism.

We have to emphasize expressly the fact that merely political democracy, that is, a certain form of state in which the government of the republic is entrusted to a parliament chosen in a general election, in no way necessarily keeps the state from falling into totalitarianism and violating the sacred rights of the individual person. A politically democratic state can easily become totalitarian. And if then the human rights of the individual are violated by the state, what difference does it make whether this violation was committed by a single person or by a majority? The suffering of the individual is equally great, as is the wickedness in the eyes of God.

It hardly needs to be mentioned that the Church understands the value of the individual person, and the superiority of the immortal soul of the individual over any natural community. The teaching of holy Church represents the most extreme antithesis to any totalitarian spirit, and she has anathematized the idolatry of the state.

But what interests us here is the question of how far the Church can be democratic in her structure in that second sense of democracy which is opposed to authoritarian procedures. And here we encounter the ridiculous demand that in our democratic time the Church be made democratic in her external structure, in her Canon Law, and in her administration. One overlooks the radical difference between the holy Church and natural communities such as the state; one is hindered by secularization and this-worldliness from seeing that what is possible, and perhaps even justified and desirable in the structure and administration of the state, is impossible in the Church and would contradict her meaning and nature and thus be a catastrophic evil. The holy Church is "authoritarian" because of her supernatural divine origin, although this term takes on here a completely new meaning, quite different from its meaning when applied to the state.

The authority of the Church is sacred. All genuine authority, whether of parents or of the state, is a partial representation of God. But in the case of the Church the representation of God is not just grounded in the kind of community which the Church is; it was explicitly established by Christ, the Son of God. His words, "You are Peter and upon this rock I will build my Church," as well as the words which follow and are addressed to the Apostles, "Whatever you will bind on earth, will be bound in heaven . . . ," show clearly the direct, explicit authority which God has committed to the Church, and which gives her a sacred character which no natural authority has. This authority is situated in areas completely different from those in which natural authorities are situated, in areas which as such have a sacred character. But above all the representation of God in the Church is totally different from any other representation of God, and is incomparably more direct than any other. This direct sacred authority has an absolute character. Especially the theoretical authority of the holy Church as the one who proclaims and protects the revelation of Christ — in matters of faith and morals — has an absolute character, and excludes any democratization. No believing Catholic can doubt that the Church has an infallible magisterium, that everything promulgated *ex cathedra* by the pope alone or with a council in matters of faith or morals, is absolutely true. As soon as some proclamation in matters of faith or morals is *de fide,* then we say, *Roma locuta, causa finita* (Rome has spoken, the matter is closed).

In the case of practical (as distinguished from theoretical) authority, which refers, for instance, to the ordinances of the pope, the protection of the Holy Spirit is not promised in the same way. Ordinances can be unfortunate, ill-conceived, even disastrous, and there have been many such in the history of the Church. Here the *Roma locuta, causa finita* does not hold. The faithful are not obliged to regard all ordinances as good and desirable. They can regret them and pray that they be taken back; indeed, they can work, with all due respect for the pope, for their elimination. But as long as such ordinances stand the faithful must obey them unless they violate the moral law and thus offend God.

This practical authority, too, is limited to certain areas; the representation of God is here, too, a partial one; this authority has a limited competence which may not be exceeded. But it, too, is essentially authoritarian, and every attempt to democratize this practical authority is wrong, and just betrays that one has lost the sense of what is the true essence of the Church. The idea that one can make the Church more accessible to the spirit of the times by this "democratization," or that this "democratization" represents improvement, has sometimes a pernicious, sometimes a naive character — but it is always an illusion. One can call for the democratization of the holy Church only if one has lost all sense for the true nature of this sacred institution. Only if the Church were merely a humanitarian institution, if her main task were limited to this world, to a realization of the ideal of Auguste Comte, could one meaningfully speak of a democratization.

But the authoritarian character of the structure of the Church should never lead to the idea that physical force can be used to bring about submission to her. Any physical force is contrary to the nature of the holy Church. The physical force which the state, even the democratic state, unavoidably uses, contradicts the nature of ecclesiastical authority. It makes sense, and is possible, to compel respect for state law by means of physical power — but it is totally wrong to want to compel the faith in others. First of all, external force cannot succeed in compelling the faith; and secondly, it is clearly wrong and displeasing to God to try to do this. Even if this has happened in the history of holy Church, it has not happened because she was too authoritarian and undemocratic, but because some of her members, caught up in a naturalistic mentality, did not see clearly enough the radical difference between a natural community, such as the state, and the holy Church. Their intention was in itself noble — they had a burning zeal for the eternal salvation of their fellow man. But they tried to achieve conversion by unsuitable means, and in the process they were even betrayed into doing what is morally wrong.

NOTES

70. Cardinal Journet, as well as Jacques Maritain in his last book, have discussed the difference between the Church as the bride of Christ, as herself a person, on the one hand, and the individual human members of the Church, on the other. The Church has never sinned, however many of her members have seriously sinned, including not only laymen but also members of the clergy and even popes. But our subject here is a different one.

21

Fear of Using the Authority of the Holy Church

THE DESIRE TO DEMOCRATIZE the Church is linked with a fear of using that authority which God has given her.

Earlier in this book, in the chapter, "The Lethargy of the Custodians," we discussed the fear of using legitimate authority. Now we have to come back to this subject in connection with the unfortunate democratization of the Church. For the present disrepute in which authority finds itself is related to the idolization of democracy. Respect for democracy has become so great that authority as such has become suspect. But the more true authority is defamed, then the more young persons fall prey to pseudo-authority, that is, the more they submit blindly to some demagogue. They are like those people who want to have nothing to do with medical doctors — and then fall into the hands of quacks. But the hostility of modern youth to authority is an age-old phenomenon. Long ago Plato said, in his dialogue *The Laws,* that the youth of his time think that they have nothing to learn, and that they refuse to accept anything from their parents.

But this hostility of children towards the authority of their parents and of their schools, their raving for revolutions, strikes, public protests, is much less dangerous than that fear of using authority which we find in many persons to whom legitimate authority has been entrusted. This fear comes partly from a respect for the (wrongly understood) freedom of others, partly from fear of public opinion — one doesn't want to appear unpopular, reactionary — partly from general human respect, often from weakness and an antipathy to acting in an "unfriendly" way, and sometimes simply from cowardice, as we saw in Chapter I. Those who for one or more of these reasons fail to use their authority often try to excuse themselves by saying, "Authority no longer works today."

Unfortunately this fear of using authority has even penetrated into the holy Church and has influenced many bishops and religious superiors. Needless to say, this fear of using authority is incomparably more irresponsible and more harmful in the Church than any place else. I was recently told by the general of a great order in the Church, who himself, at least at the time when I spoke to him, deplored some of the bad trends within the clergy and saw something of the devastation of the vineyard of the Lord: "What can I do; authority is no longer effective today. We rather have to take the attitude of a St. Monica — pray, weep, and have patience."

There are many errors contained in this statement. First of all, it is by no means true that authority has lost its effectiveness. A superior today can still suspend a member of his order, forbid him to teach, or even expel him from the order. He can use his authority just as effectively as the director of a hospital would use his in dismissing some of his doctors if they were incompetent, or were using patients for experiments. A religious superior is responsible for not using his authority, and his responsibility is much greater than that of Eli in the Old Testament. It is simply not true that the authority of a superior is no longer effective. The comparison with St. Monica can only be applied to the conversion of someone. It is totally inapplicable if it is a question of restraining someone from poisoning the souls of others, of using authority to prevent someone from inflicting this wrong on others. In this case a superior can and must intervene. He can do this today as well as in any other era; and if he does nothing, he acts like the hireling of which our Lord speaks.

The use of legitimate, God-given authority is never felt to be pleasant by one who, though under authority, is filled with a revolutionary spirit. Usually a child will inwardly rebel when his parents forbid him something, but that does not keep the child from obeying, even if unwillingly. This unwillingness to submit to authority — however legitimate and God-given the authority is — is rooted in fallen human nature, and is to be found in all eras. And so the assertion is false that authority is ineffective today when exercised by legitimate superiors. As far as formal intervention goes, such as suspending or expelling someone, the use of authority is thoroughly effective, especially the authority of bishops and religious superiors. We do not deny that resistance to authority and unwillingness to obey is especially prominent today and is fostered by all kinds of demagogues (and quite often by Communist agents who are themselves slaves of a brutal and illegitimate totalitarian authority). But the failure to use the authority which has been given by God in a special way, really comes from human respect, from feeling more responsible to public opinion than to Christ, and from the fact that one fears the reputation of being reactionary more than the offense against God which lies in not using the authority which derives from Him, and fears this reputation more than harm to souls. Now this, too, is a result of this-worldliness.

Of course revolutionary propaganda and the spirit of the times can make it more difficult than in earlier times to intervene effectively with authority. But is this a reason for making cowardly compromises? On the other hand, the consequences of suspension or expulsion from an order are not nearly so bad for him who is suspended or expelled as in earlier times: he will be celebrated by the liberal world, honored, given the aura of a "martyr" for freedom.

The right use of the sacred authority of a bishop or a religious superior is much more necessary, more urgently called for by God when it is not just the deviation of an individual which is at stake, but rather the spreading of a terrible spiritual plague by one who is either malicious or ignorant. The failure to use God-given authority against such a person is a *betrayal* of Christ. Anyone who, from cowardice or insufficient moral courage, fails to take up a fight, brings a terrible responsibility upon himself.

This failure to use God-given authority when God is clearly calling a bishop or a superior to use it, is, as one can easily see, linked with worldliness and to the distorted idea of love of neighbor. All authoritative intervention is seen in the light of a lack of love and respect for the person of the one who is disciplined. Let us grant that authority was often misused in earlier times — whether the authority of parents, of religious superiors, of priests in confession, and sometimes even of bishops — nevertheless today's failure to use God-given authority in no way overcomes the earlier abuses of authority, but rather derives from the same basic attitude: from the loss of a truly supernatural spirit. There is, of course, the danger that a person who has authority will abuse it. And here we are thinking not just of that abuse which comes from exceeding the competence of a given authority and interfering with things which lie beyond the sphere of that authority. We are especially thinking of the psychological danger which a great God-given position of authority has for many persons, including noble and devout persons: starting with a sense of responsibility for the use of their authority, they run the danger of regarding their own opinion as infallible, and of losing sight of the difference between administering their office in a supernatural spirit, and simply indulging their own authoritarian dispositions. To lapse from zeal, which is subjectively noble and filled with a sense of responsibility, into servitude to an authoritarian disposition, which is simply rooted in one's nature, is a form of naturalism, a loss of the sense for the supernatural. This was the tragedy of Pope Paul IV, Carafa.

The betrayal of God-given authority, by keeping silent or by not intervening where this is a sacred duty before God, is always a very grave fault. Sometimes it comes from the ostrich-policy of burying one's head in the sand and not wanting to see the evils which authority *can* and should eliminate; sometimes it comes from the slogan, "Authority is no longer effective today, it belongs to the Middle Ages." This is much more dangerous than the abuse of authority which we just discussed; it is an even worse naturalism than this abuse, it is a failure to see what is demanded by the sacred office of a bishop or a religious superior. One looks upon authority as uncharitable and harsh because one looks at it "from without," and fails to understand that it is a deed of the greatest love, that it is true love of neighbor to use God-given authority in the spirit of Christ and with the full awareness of being responsible before God.

Thank God there are still many orthodox bishops who fight courageously against the devastation of the vineyard of the Lord. They have the real courage of a Christian confessor. They are all the more to be admired because so many other bishops do not have this courage, and because their effective intervention is made much more difficult by the new bureaucracy in the Church and its "legalism." For by establishing national councils of bishops, individual bishops are made dependent on the majorities of these councils in a way which often hinders them from acting and intervening according to their conscience. Then there are the priests' councils, which in the name of democracy often make it more difficult for the bishops to act, and parish councils, which often hinder orthodox pastors from carrying on their struggle against "progressivism."

The energetic struggle against the ever-increasing work of Satan to undermine the holy Church from within demands not only holy courage — it also demands a burning faith in Christ and His holy Church, a faith which is not to be shaken by any trend of the time, by any number of books by well-known theologians (some of whom were orthodox before the Council), by the press and public opinion.

It is clear what great strength of faith is required for martyrdom. To be ready to die for the true Faith reveals an immense strength of faith. There are so many degrees of faith, and doubt is not one of them, not even the lowest. No, doubt is not a weak stage of faith, but the absence of faith, as Cardinal Newman shows clearly. And it is even more an absence of faith if someone, while not denying the content of faith, thinks that it is as likely to be true as to be false, or if someone says, "Perhaps it is true that Christ is the Son of God, but how can this be known for sure." But if someone is tormented by doubts and fights against them, he might very well have the true faith. The great Kierkegaard has said many beautiful and important things on this type of faith.

But in speaking of degrees of faith, we are here thinking of something quite different. The first degree of faith is found when one's faith is still strongly supported by the social surroundings in which one lives; it is a faith which is too dependent on tradition and almost a matter of convention. We pass through countless degrees in the strength of one's faith as we mount up from this faith to the faith which we find in Pascal's *Mémorial,* in Cardinal Mindszenty, who submitted to all kinds of torture rather than renounce one iota of his faith, and finally up to the faith of the martyr St. Ignatius of Antioch.

The present time demands that the bishops, the "good shepherds," possess faith in a high degree. Here we are not thinking of holy courage, of strength and stature of personality, but rather of strength and absoluteness of faith, of the readiness to defend the true Faith *opportune importune* (in season and out of season) against all distortions, however hidden they might be. We are thinking of the strength and absoluteness of faith which makes one immune to the uncanny power of tendencies of the time — to those ideas which fill the air and present themselves as healthy and necessary evolution, and which make all protest against them appear to be the protest of an "angry old man," of someone who is caught up in habit and is incapable of receiving new life.

And here we encounter today an extremely curious phenomenon: there are delicate personality-types who are not at all militant by nature, but who have a deep faith and would be ready to die as martyrs in a persecution — yet they are unable to oppose the bad trends of the time within the Church and the many false prophets.

22

False Interpretation of Authority

IN AN EARLIER WORK we distinguished genuine authority from any merely functional authority (*Die Menschheit am Scheideweg*). There is a certain relation between a superior and a subordinate which results from a contract. This is a practical, technical authority which is indispensable for the functioning of a factory, a hospital, or any organization in which a number of people work together. This authority is legitimate only when the subordinate binds himself to his superior; thus it was certainly wrong when in earlier times men were forced to work for others. But as I showed in this earlier writing of mine, we must clearly distinguish this functional authority from real and genuine authority, which derives its right to command from the fact that it is a partial representation of God. Such is the authority of parents or of the state. Whether we are speaking of the authority of a king, or of a president or a parliament chosen in a general election, this authority always comes from "above" and involves a partial representation of God; this is in contrast to any merely functional authority. It would be contrary to the nature of true authority if its sphere of competence were now broader, now narrower. The decrees and laws of true authority are not binding simply because the individual has explicitly committed himself to them. As I tried to show in my earlier work, real authority is one of the genuine sources of moral obligation, and it is something quite striking that a decree is binding for an individual simply because it has been issued by a legitimate authority.

We refer to these facts here because Karl Rahner, in a lecture at the Catholic Academy in Munich, has spoken of a reinterpretation of authority. This lecture contains elementary philosophical errors, which betray a surprising blindness to the difference between sacred and profane authority.

It is more than regrettable that Rahner remarked that the previous notion of authority in the Church was "feudalistic," or rather suitable only for a feudalistic society and no longer for "modern" man. The same man who twenty years ago wrote significant theological works has now fallen prey to a distinctly mediocre "sociologization," an unfortunate fashion of the times. There is an analogy between Rahner's position and the position expressed by the slogan, "We have to liberate ourselves from the Greek mentality, from the Platonic error that there is an objective truth." It is a childish error to think that ultimate fundamental realities — which one unavoidably reintroduces as soon as one tries to deny them — are nothing but expressions of a nation, an era, or a sociological structure. And the research of a scientific sociology presupposes all these fundamental realities such as objective truth. There is an analogy to this attempt to make truth a function of the Greek mentality, in Rahner's assertion that so basic a reality as genuine authority is nothing but the product of a particular sociological structure such as feudalism. This is an unfortunate and self-contradictory error. And this error is all the more astonishing coming from a theologian, for it betrays a blindness to the fundamental reality of the authority of God, which is the *causa exemplaris* (ideal model) of all authority.

If this lecture of Rahner is conspicuous for lapsing into mediocre "sociologizing," it is also conspicuous for its confusion regarding the nature of authority. The nature of a datum so central and fundamental as authority is crudely misunderstood. What is in reality true authority should according to Rahner be "abolished," and replaced by a purely functional authority. But the worst of Rahner's lecture is yet a third point: the failure to distinguish between sacred and profane authority. In trying to eliminate everything "paternalistic" in Church authority, he is trying to desacralize Church authority and to eliminate the essential difference between sacred and profane authority. Indeed, he would thereby reduce sacred authority to profane authority, and not just to true profane authority, but to neutral, purely technical functional authority — to authority without strength and dignity. Is he aware of the consequences which this has for that obedience which we owe to sacred authority?

Why this fear of fatherhood, when God again and again in the Gospel calls Himself our Heavenly Father? In the prayer which Christ taught us, almighty God, the Creator of heaven and earth, the infinitely holy, unapproachable God is addressed as our Father; why then does Rahner protest that the vicar of Christ on earth, the successor of the prince of the Apostles, should no longer call us his beloved sons and daughters?

This reinterpretation of the authority of the holy Church is not a new interpretation of authority, but rather simply a misunderstanding of the basic reality of sacred authority. It is as if someone were to fail to see the difference between a college professor and a doctor of the Church. Rahner would eliminate the greatness and dignity of the authority of a bishop or a superior, as well as the holy, fatherly love which permeates it; he would replace the glory of the unique direct bond with God through Christ, with a dull, flat, purely earthly relation which lacks real supernatural love. He fails to distinguish the different kinds of authority as well as the different categories of love, such as fatherly love, love of neighbor, love for an exemplary person, etc.

All authority attaches to an office and not to the person who holds the office. But the love which goes with sacred authority and which is grounded in the office of this sacred authority necessarily has a paternal character, just as obedience to sacred authority includes an element of filial love. We should never sacrifice all these timeless basic realities and basic truths to the mythical modern man — who lives only in the phantasy of sociologists. Soon we will hear that it is intolerable for "modern" man to be born of parents.

This reinterpretation of authority represents, unfortunately, not a private opinion of Karl Rahner, but a widespread tendency. It is also a result of this-worldliness, of a loss of the sense for the supernatural, and of that desacralization or secularization which goes hand in hand with this. And this-worldliness is not only incompatible with the teaching of the holy Church and the Revelation of Christ, but with any kind of religion.

23
The Catchword "Ghetto"

ALTHOUGH THE STATEMENT, "The Church must abandon
the ghetto in which she has imprisoned herself for so long,"
is a very effective slogan (as are most slogans), in reality
it contains many grave and primitive errors (as do most
slogans). It would be an interesting philosophical task to
investigate the nature of the slogan as such and to show the
basis of that illegitimate effectiveness which is characteristic
of it. In *The Trojan Horse* I have already referred to this, but
it would be worth the trouble to say more about this dangerous intellectual weapon and its insidious effectiveness. It
is astonishing how naively and gullibly slogans are accepted —
and how easily they can vilify even very good things. Unfortunately we cannot here analyze the nature of the slogan
as such, but we can analyze the various dangerous errors
which are contained in the catchword "Catholic ghetto."

If by "ghetto" one means the glorious fortress of truth
which the Church has been for two thousand years in with-

standing all errors of the times and heresies, then the word is used in a distinctly foolish and stupid way. A ghetto was an area in which Jews, more or less against their will, had to live separated from the rest of the world. This original notion of ghetto has led today to the negative connotation of being severed from the rest of the world, of being narrow-minded, and intellectually and spiritually primitive.

Of course there is a certain narrowness which has sometimes characterized Catholics, for instance in philosophy. Many Catholic philosophers have thought that they could philosophize only as strict Thomists. Instead of asking whether something is true, they have asked where it fits in the Thomist system. I have dealt with this narrowness in many of my writings, and most recently in *The Trojan Horse,* Chapter 6 — while at the same time always emphasizing that not just any philosophy is compatible with Christianity, that many philosophies are destructive of Christianity. And then there is the very different kind of narrowness which has sometimes characterized Catholics and which I have opposed all my life in many writings — a false supernaturalism which fails to understand the God-given mission of natural goods and tends to see them in the light of merely worldly goods. But the progressivists who call the Church a ghetto do not have these forms of narrowness in mind, for the secularization and this-worldliness which they also advocate in no way correct this narrowness, as we have shown. No, they are in reality comparing the Church with a ghetto because she has been impenetrable by heresy, gloriously sealed off from all error. Now this use of the catchword "ghetto" betrays a host of grave and foolish errors.

Truth is the source of all real breadth and universality. Error is a prison of the spirit, and it radiates an oppressive narrowness. True breadth and openness of spirit in the realm of philosophy or religion does not lie in pluralism but in clearly recognizing and being grounded in the exclusiveness of truth. Just as it is no sign of breadth or openness of mind when one fails to distinguish clearly between good and evil, and when one relativizes all morality, so it is no sign of openness of mind to fail to grasp the exclusiveness of truth.

Relativism and openness of mind exclude one another. Just as stubbornness betrays narrowness of spirit because of its lack of objectivity and its pseudo-security, which is not grounded in real reasons, so relativism is a catastrophic self-deception for failing to submit to the call of reality, for feeling superior, free, and independent in this lack of objectivity. Relativism is specifically narrow because of its lack of objectivity, and it imprisons itself in itself in a special way by cutting itself off from the "logos" of being. It must be said once and for all: it is self-contradictory to be open-minded to error. It is like praising a susceptibility for disease as a particular sign of health. No, only the truth makes us free and lets us participate in real universality. It is a special sign of this freedom and universality, and of openmindedness, to be immune to error, especially to philosophical and metaphysical error, and pre-eminently to heresy, to any teaching incompatible with the divine Revelation of Christ. This is precisely the unique universality of the Church — and catholic means universal — and this is why she is the protector of the divine Revelation, why she is immune to any heresy, why she is a fortress of truth with impenetrable walls. She is the very antithesis to the countless real ghettoes of the spirit, such as the ghetto of error, of prejudice, of lack of objectivity, of immanentism, of relativism, of the spirit of the times, of fashion, of nationalism, etc.

24
Cooperation with Atheists?

But sometimes one even says that the Church should abandon her ghetto and not only work ecumenically with members of other religions but with atheists — whether Marxist or not — for a better world, for a more humane existence for the individual. Here one does not apply the term "ghetto" to the Church as a fortress of truth, but to the Church's supposed detachment from non-Catholics in the attempt to solve the great problems which go with building a better world. One reproaches the Church — whether rightly or wrongly remains to be seen — with being indifferent to humanizing the world, and with refusing to work with non-Catholics on this urgent task.

To deal with this reproach, and to determine how much cooperation with atheists is possible, we must first of all make clear the meaning of humanization, for this word can be understood in very different ways.

If by humanization one means the struggle against poverty, the introduction of hygienic living conditions — in a word, a purely external improvement of civilization (as distinguished from culture) — then of course Catholics can work with atheists on projects of humanization. But it is carrying coals to Newcastle to urge this — it is something which has for a long time been taken for granted in politics. Social democrats and Catholics formed for years a coalition in the Weimar Republic. What hinders cooperation for this kind of humanization are the distinctly economic interests of parties, as well as conflicting sociological theories, but not religious and basic philosophical questions.

But even this kind of cooperation is impossible with Communists — for they are not really interested in improving the economic condition of man, but in spreading the Communist system. It is truly a naive optimism, which sees everything through rose-colored glasses, to think that real Communists have an interest in the welfare of the individual. Every other interest than absolute loyalty to the party is for them unthinkable; absolute slave-like obedience to the party is their *only* interest. Any pity, any interest for anything which would contradict, or in any way even harm the party, is looked on as wrong, as a weakness not to be tolerated. Whoever thinks that we could have an objective dialogue with a convinced Communist, and that the Communist would consider what we say from the point of view of truth, betrays great ignorance as to the nature of Communism. But of course one could vote with the Communists of a country for building for instance a highway, or one could vote in the United Nations with a Communist country like China against Russia on some question, or vice versa. But it is a sheer illusion to imagine that a common basis of fundamental agreement could be found with Communists for a humanitarian improvement of the world even with regard to quite external material goods.[71]

But what is much more important in our context is the false but widespread notion of humanization. In this notion one often identifies basic material improvements in the life of the individual (such as the absence of war) with the full natural development of the person and his true earthly happiness.

Now it is true that real humanization includes struggling against the systematic depersonalization and dehumanization which dominate today's world. We have already discussed this in detail in speaking of the illusion of progress in the modern world. The struggle against dehumanization includes especially the struggle against collectivism, against all illegitimate modes of influence (such as brain-washing), against any totalitarian intervention by the state, against the destruction of organic forms of human life and community, as well as of the intimate sphere of the individual person, against the tendency to make everything uniform, — against impurity, and shamelessness. How can we work for this humanization with men who neither believe in Christ, nor recognize Christian morality? How can we work with atheists towards this true humanization of the world — we should rather say *re*-humanization? We are not thinking here just of Marxist atheists — for then it would be absurd even to pose this question at all.

Even prescinding from Marxism, the notion of atheism remains very ambiguous. By an atheist we could mean a man who has not yet found God, but who would be happy if he could believe in God. Or we could mean the very different type of man who cannot stand the idea of the living God, who would say with Dietrich Kerler, "Even if you could prove mathematically that God exists, I would still not want Him to exist since He would limit my own metaphysical stature." With this latter type, who prefers that there be no God, it is clearly impossible to work together toward the real humanization of mankind even from a natural point of view. If someone in no way realizes the transcendence of man, that man is created for something beyond himself (such was the view of Diderot, who said that there is nothing greater for man than man), and even more if someone feels his pride to be especially satisfied by his atheism, then he is simply incapable of understanding the real nature of man, the sources of true happiness, or the evil of depersonalization. It would be an extremely naive illusion to want to work with such men towards authentic humanization. There can be no cooperation with a Nietzsche in working towards humanization.

Of course there are certain individual matters on which we can work with those atheists who are really searching for God, who would be happy if they could believe in God, who recognize the transcendence of man, and who suffer under their inability to find an object for man's metaphysical drive to transcend himself. But all those atheists who replace God with "mankind" or the "totality" have already distorted man's real transcendence. Precisely with such persons it is utterly impossible to cooperate in working toward true humanization. In place of man's transcendence they have put a distortion of the individual person, a pseudo-courage, which as we saw satisfies man's pride by making him feel that he is a part of a larger whole. But even with "tragic" atheists — I would call them searching atheists — the cooperation which is possible in working for true humanization is very limited.

But if we turn to a Socrates, who could never be called an

atheist, then there would be a broad field of possible cooperation; yet as we will see now, Socrates is no longer possible today.

Unlike purely external welfare, real humanization can never be attained by external means such as laws of the state. It demands instead thorough education, deep changes in attitudes toward life, a rediscovery of the true sources of human happiness. And at this point the question must be raised: is such a deep cure of mankind — for the terrible depersonalization of our time is a grave disease — possible at all without Christ? Can an unredeemed mankind overcome this disease? Does this not require the help of grace? Has one forgotten the reality of the fall of man? And of course we were speaking above only of a natural earthly humanization, and not of the fulfilment of the real destiny of man which lies in glorifying God by personal holiness, and in attaining to eternal happiness. But even if we limit ourselves to the question of a cure on the purely natural level for that depersonalization which is spreading today, we have to ask whether this is possible without Christ, without the new principle of supernatural life which we receive in baptism, without the true moral teaching of the Church.

Here we touch upon the great question of whether the natural watchful waiting of mankind before the coming of Christ, is still possible after He has come? Is a Socrates still possible today? Is this high natural humanity still possible today after Christ has illuminated the world with a completely new light? "He who is not with me is against me": Socrates did not yet face this alternative. Can we hope today to attain even a natural rehumanization without Christ? (Kierkegaard has expressed all this in distinguishing between the pagan and the apostate.) It is in this light that the question of cooperation with non-believers and with those who do not accept Christian morality, must be considered.

But much more important in our context is the fatal fact that this-worldliness has obscured in many people's minds the difference between an external improvement of the world and of the external conditions of life on the one hand, and real natural humanization on the other. At the same time — and this is incomparably worse — one no longer sees the absolute primacy which the glorification of God, transformation in Christ, and eternal blessedness, have over the highest earthly humanization. But as we saw above, true and valid humanization is possible only when this primacy is fully understood. Without God, without Christ, without the redemption of Christ, without love for Christ, without the new supernatural principle of life bestowed in baptism, there can be no ultimate natural fulfilment of man and no real earthly happiness.

NOTES

71. In speaking here of cooperation with atheists we mean a systematic program of cooperation, and not merely a concurrence in voting on individual concrete questions in a parliament or at the United Nations. This latter is of course possible with anyone, no matter what his convictions or motives might be. In the Italian parliament the Communists once voted with the Christian Democrats to recognize the Catholic Church as the religion of the state. In such a vote the question of motives of course plays no role. But this occasional political concurrence, which has something almost accidental about it, is clearly not a program of cooperation in which everyone aims at the same goal, and is motivated by the same reasons.

25

Harmless Religion

ONE OF THE MOST unfortunate results of this-worldliness is that even in the Church real hope is more and more replaced by optimism. One passes over in silence the metaphysical tragedy of man, his weakness in observing the laws of God, his susceptibility for sin, the necessity of dying, the judgment of God, which is magnificently presented to us in the *Dies Irae*. One thinks that this world is a "vale of tears" only because it contains poverty, social injustice, disease — in other words for purely earthly reasons and not because of the metaphysical situation of man. The spirit of this-worldliness even pushes into the background the deepest suffering which we can experience on earth, the death of a beloved person.

We find even in the new liturgy a sad expression of this mediocre attempt to hide the seriousness of the metaphysical situation of man. One has deprived the Mass for the Dead, the Requiem, of its great solemnity, one has eliminated the *Dies*

Irae and has even added the Alleluia.[72] But this suppresses the human aspect of death, which is after all something terrible, and a punishment for the fall. The grief which is motivated by the human aspect of death is not simply eliminated by the fact that we have been redeemed by Christ, and that death can be the entrance to eternal blessedness. Even in the light of faith death remains something ultimately serious, indeed something to be feared, because in it we encounter the judgment of God. It remains the great moment of decision. A supernatural view of death discloses the majesty of God, the great importance of the fate of every human soul, the ultimate significance of holiness and sin. The joy of the Alleluia is here artificial, ungenuine — it not only distorts the moment in which everything is at stake for man, it also deprives the Alleluia of its true blissful ring. It is in general a great mistake to jump over and to suppress the human aspect of things, and to pretend that the Christian sees only the supernatural aspect of things. For this would not be a triumph of faith, or even a false supernaturalism, but rather, curiously, a result of this-worldliness and of losing sight of supernatural reality.

To see the purely human aspect of things is a necessary foundation for seeing the supernatural aspect. One who does not see the human aspect is insensitive and superficial, and his attitude is incompatible with the true faith. The deeper one sees the natural tragedy of death, then the more one is able to grasp the tremendous significance of our redemption through Christ, and the more one possesses that true faith which St. Paul expresses by asking, "O death, where is your sting?" But as soon as one jumps over the human aspect without passing through it, one does not ascend to the supernatural aspect, but rather replaces the natural with the supernatural aspect, which can only be attained by faith — one treats the supernatural aspect as if it were the natural, one takes it for granted, and omits that *sursum corda,* that ascent into the supernatural world which is possible only in faith. If the human aspect is not duly seen, then the aspect of faith is naturalized, and dragged down to the level of the obvious. If the human aspect is suppressed or omitted, then the aspect of faith becomes ungenuine, unreal.

Thus the Alleluia and the elimination of black vestments in the Requiem not only ignores the human aspect of death, but also distorts the supernatural perspective on death. The death of a man is the moment of judgment, it is the great and fearful encounter with the divine Judge. Although death is transfigured by hope — hope for our dead beloved one, and for all who loved him and mourn for him — this hope does not take away ultimate seriousness and holy fear. It is simply not the right form for the Mass for the Dead when this Mass gives the impression of celebrating the entrance of the deceased into eternal blessedness. How, then, does the Mass for the Dead differ from a feast day in honor of a saint, of whom we know in faith that he has entered into eternal blessedness?

The optimism of the new Mass for the Dead, as well as its tendency to introduce a harmless note into the theme of the judgment of God (there was none of this in the Tridentine Requiem) is deeply related to this-worldliness, and to a loss of a sense of the supernatural.

This-worldliness leads to yet other expressions of harmlessness in religion. Long before Vatican II there was the danger of religion becoming harmless, bourgeois, conventional. Opposition to conventionalism in religion was to be the work of the Council. But unfortunately an effort was made to overcome this conventionalism and harmlessness by *aggiornamento* — by adapting to "modern man." The hope was that especially in the post-conciliar period, religion could be given new vitality by being plunged into the rhythm of daily life — but the result was not only a failure to sanctify daily life, but a deeper and deeper lapse into a desacralization of religion.

The danger of harmlessness in religion is deeply rooted in human nature. Kierkegaard waged a magnificent and relentless war against the attempts of Danish Protestantism to render the Christian Revelation harmless. And we find Newman waging this same war before his entrance into the Catholic Church as well as after. In one of his Anglican sermons, he begins by speaking of the religious danger of earlier, more primitive times: "The age was rude and fierce. Satan took the darker side of the Gospel: its awful mysteriousness, its fearful glory, its sovereign inflexible justice; and here *his* picture of the truth ended, 'God is a consuming fire.' " Then Newman turns to the present and asks: "What is Satan's device in this day? A far different one; but perhaps a more pernicious. He has taken the brighter side of the Gospel — its tidings of comfort, its precepts of love; all darker, deeper views of man's condition and prospects being comparatively forgotten. This is the religion *natural* to a civilized age, and well has Satan dressed and completed it into an idol of the Truth. . . . Religion is pleasant and easy; benevolence is the chief virtue; intolerance, bigotry, excess of zeal, are the first of sins."[73]

Holy Fear

If in Kierkegaard's time conventionalism and harmlessness took the form of making Christianity acceptable to fashionable society, today it takes the form of destroying the

ultimate seriousness of our situation before God, of lapsing
into a harmless optimism, of suppressing all fear of God, all
trembling at the thought of the day of judgment. This is
something incomparably worse than the pre-conciliar conventionalism. We have already mentioned the ostrich-policy
with respect to the tragedy of death viewed in its human
aspect, and to the tremendous seriousness of the judgment
which awaits us after death. But we constantly encounter
today in many other ways this blindness for the seriousness
of man's metaphysical situation. Although Christ so often
speaks of hell, of the narrowness of the way which leads to
heaven, of the guest who was not dressed in a wedding
garment, and although He has said, "Many are called but
few are chosen," nevertheless we hear so little of all this
today in sermons, pastoral letters, and even in encyclicals.

It is only to be expected that the fear of God is more or
less forgotten when the main emphasis is transferred from
the "things which are above," as St. Paul says (Col. 3:2),
to earthly progress — to the relief of earthly needs and sufferings, and the elimination of poverty and war. When one
renders the supernatural harmless, so as not to be distracted
in one's work of improving the world, or in the cheerful,
optimistic development of one's natural powers, then one
tries to eliminate the cross from the life of the Christian. In
fact one avoids even mentioning the existence of hell in
sermons, catechisms, pastoral letters — and thus it is quite
consistent to avoid mentioning holy fear.

Holy fear and trembling in the presence of the incomprehensible greatness and holiness of God, which is to be sharply
distinguished from slavish fear, is an essential element of any
real religion. Holy fear goes far beyond the response of reverence, which is so centrally important. It was holy fear which

led St. Peter to say, "Lord, depart from me, for I am a sinful man"; and it is holy fear which Rudolph Otto has in mind in speaking of God as *mysterium tremendum*. This fear is a value response to God. It is a centrally important religious act, and without it there is no real religion at all.[74]

But there is another holy fear which is a response to God as judge and which plays a prominent role in the Judeo-Christian Revelation. This fear is bound up with our awareness of being sinners and of having to answer to the divine Judge. Love of God in and through Christ indeed goes far beyond this response of holy fear, but not by excluding it, or simply replacing it. The more one loves God, the more one responds with holy fear to His unapproachable majesty — and to Him as Judge. Of course this holy fear of the day of judgment is permeated by hope and love and faith in our redemption through Christ, but it is never replaced by a false security. Real love for God presupposes fear; there is no love of God without real fear of God.

Of course love for God drives out slavish fear, but *never* true holy fear of God. Love goes gloriously beyond this holy fear, but not by eliminating it. We find something similar in the relation between obedience and love: love of God goes far beyond mere obedience, it is something quite new with respect to obedience, but it does not eliminate obedience — quite the contrary, love presupposes obedience and strengthens our will to obey. Our relation to God, Who is infinitely holy and the absolute Lord, must be one filled with adoration and trembling reverence. But while we are on earth we must also fear God as Judge, and fear the loss of eternal union with Him whom we love above all else. The *Dies Irae* expresses this fear of God: *"Rex tremendae majestatis qui salvandos salvas gratis: salva me fons pietatis"* (O

King of fearful majesty, You Who save the elect without any merit of their own, save me in your unfathomable merciful love). But this holy fear of God, in which we become aware of the great seriousness of our situation before God, does not lead to a gloomy self-preoccupation, or to constant restlessness and anxiety; it is rather united, in and through Christ, with blissful hope and love.

Holy Zeal

Turning to a related subject: we find a further sign of this-worldliness in the disappearance of burning zeal for the glorification of God, for the imitation of Christ, and for His holy Church. In the Introduction to his *Rule,* St. Benedict distinguishes between good zeal, and the zeal of bitterness. Today there is truly no lack of the zeal of bitterness — every Communist agent is an example of an evil zeal which is matchless. But even in the holy Church we find this evil zeal at a high pitch among those who want to destroy the Church, or at least make it this-worldly. We have only to think of IDOC (Information Documentation sur l'Eglise conciliaire) and of countless other powerful organizations of the radical progressivists and modernists. But burning zeal for the truth, for God, for Christ and His holy Church, is looked on as fanatical, intolerant, and incompatible with charity.

Of this burning holy zeal, which every true Christian necessarily possesses, Newman says: "Now I fear we lack altogether . . . firmness, manliness, godly severity. We are over-tender in dealing with sin and sinners. We are deficient in the jealous custody of the revealed Truths which Christ has left us. We allow men to speak against the Church, its ordinances, or its teaching, without remonstrating with them. We do not separate from heretics, nay, we object to the word as if uncharitable. . . ."[75] In another place Newman speaks in a wonderful way of the deeply Christian union of burning zeal and love: "Oh, that there was in us this high temper of mingled austerity and love! Barely do we conceive of severity by itself, and of kindness by itself; but who unites them? We think we cannot be kind without ceasing to be severe. Who is there that walks through the world, wounding according to the rule of zeal, and scattering balm in the fulness of love; smiting as a duty, and healing as a privilege; loving most when he seems sternest, and embracing them most tenderly whom in semblance he treats roughly?"[76]

In the saints we find this union of burning zeal and triumphant love of neighbor — one has only to think of the Apostles, of St. Peter, St. Paul, St. John, or of St. Athanasius, St. Augustine, St. Francis de Sales, St. Catherine of Siena, St. Theresa of Avila, and countless others.

We see another symptom of this-worldliness in this decline of burning zeal for the glorification of God and the salvation of souls, and in the increase of zeal for the improvement of the world and for what is supposedly progress. This shift of emphasis which we find even with regard to zeal is united in a terrible way with the trend to make the Christian Revelation harmless, bourgeois. This harmlessness, which Kierkegaard fought so magnificently in Danish Protestantism, and Newman in Anglican England, is, as Newman himself says, a perpetual danger. But today we find a twofold evil: harmlessness and loss of holy fear, as well as loss of burning zeal for supernatural things, have not only penetrated into the sanctuary of the Catholic Church — they even claim to be progress, to be a "triumph of tolerance" to involve "abandoning the ghetto," "overcoming superstition," etc.

NOTES

72. That the Alleluia is not prescribed for the new Mass for the Dead (but merely allowed and often sung), does not change the fact that such a Mass introduces a deplorable harmlessness into religion and a misunderstanding of the metaphysical situation of man. For this Alleluia is not an abuse which has been forbidden (as blasphemous Masses) but is sometimes tolerated by bishops; it is rather something that has been officially permitted. This holds even more for the omission of the *Dies Irae.* Today, when many "renewers" treat things which are allowed as if they were required, the fact that the Alleluia is allowed tells us a great deal about a prevailing tendency.

73. *Parochial and Plain Sermons,* vol. I, sermon 24, "The Religion of the Day." This and the following quotations from Newman are taken from an excellent article by Dr. John Crosby, "Holy Fear and Burning Zeal," *Triumph,* April, 1972.

74. Even in Eastern religions, which believe in a non-personal God, this fear is found, even if only in an analogous form. There is an element of fear in the awareness of the "sacred," which plays such a prominent role in these religions. Here, too, God is conceived as *mysterium tremendum,* although in a very different way from that of the monotheistic religions, in which God is conceived as absolute person.

75. *Parochial and Plain Sermons,* vol. II, sermon 23.

76. *Ibid.,* vol. III, sermon 13.

26

The Message of the "Our Father"

:::

IF WE HERE DARE TO SPEAK of the "Our Father" in order to show what a radical antithesis it is to this-worldliness, we fully realize how inadequate are our words about this prayer of prayers. There are after all so many interpretations by Church Fathers and other great theologians of earlier times, that it might seem arrogant of me to present the following meditations on the "Our Father." But they are necessary to show the tremendous danger of this-worldliness and its total incompatibility with the Christian revelation.

The "Our Father," the prayer which Christ taught the Apostles and of which He said, "In this way you should pray," this prayer contains in its opening words a decisive revelation. The invocation of Yahweh, the Unapproachable One, with "our Father," contains the completely new and indescribably consoling revelation that God is our Father. Our "being sheltered" (*Geborgenheit*) in God, and God's love for us, is all contained in the words, "our Father." If the greatest difference is that between a non-personal deity, and a personal God — *Deus videns et vivens* (a living God who sees us), one must nevertheless not underestimate the importance of the difference between, on the one hand, the unapproachable God, the absolute Lord, the Creator of heaven and earth, the living God into whose hands it is terrible to fall, and on the other hand God as loving Father.

But these two differences are not exactly parallel. In passing from the notion of a nonpersonal God to that of a personal God, *Deus videns et vivens,* one passes from darkness to light, and overcomes a great error. For God, who is the absolute being, is *not* non-personal — a non-personal being could never be absolute. But in calling upon God as "our Father," it remains true that He is the Unapproachable One, the Judge to be feared, One who fills us with fear and trembling. None of this is eliminated but is rather transcended and crowned by the fact, so consoling and so overwhelming, that God is also a loving Father, that our relation to Him is not only only that of a slave and servant but also that of a child. This is analagous to the relation between obedience and love. Obedience to God is never overthrown by love for God, but remains of great importance. Something new and still more sublime is added. We always remain slaves and servants of God, even if we are His children.

But right after the inexhaustibly glorious message of the invocation "our Father," there come the words, "who art in heaven." This calls to mind the unspeakably mysterious glory of God. After the intimacy which lies in the invocation "our Father," we are freed from the danger of becoming too familiar with God. The incomprehensible mysteriousness of Him who is enthroned above the world, His transcendence, is clearly expressed in the words, "who art in heaven." Here we see that true prayer is characterized by a looking up to heavenly things, a vertical "direction" (which Teilhard would replace by a horizontal "direction"). And these important words in the invocation, "who art in heaven," should be prayed by us. Praying is after all not just an observing, but a turning to God; these words involve the actualization of the attitude of a child, of looking up to Him who is enthroned above the world and reigns in heaven. It is not difficult to see that these words show once and for all that any attempt to deny the transcendence of God is radically incompatible with the Christian Revelation.

The first thing which follows is adoration, "hallowed be Thy name." This is not a prayer of petition, or of thanksgiving, or even of praise as in the *Gloria*, "laudamus te, benedicimus te." It is an act of adoring invocation. The name of God is objectively something infinitely holy. In praying "hallowed be Thy name," we enter into that rhythm of the glorification of God which objectively exists. We are not here praying that God will bring it about that everyone will adore Him, we are rather giving utterance to that which objectively ought to be as it is, and we are clearly expressing the primacy of the glorification of God.

Then follows, "Thy kingdom come." Here, too, we are primarily repeating, as it were, the "gesture" of something which objectively ought to be, we are participating in the glorification of God, and taking a primary interest in it. The kingdom of God is above all the kingdom of God in the soul of the individual, which means personal sanctification, and glorifying God as a result. But this kingdom also involves the triumph over the prince of this world; this triumph lies in the spreading of the communion of saints on earth. For we find running through the entire Gospel words such as,

"Proclaim to them the kingdom of God," and "The Kingdom of God is near."

The Old Testament prophets, especially Isaiah, speak of a kind of restitution of paradise, in which there is no more suffering and in which there is peace, even among animals. But in the New Testament it is the glorious second coming of Christ which is spoken of, the Parousia — though this second coming is not clearly distinguished from the Last Judgment, the end of the world, and the resurrection of the dead, in other words it is not distinguished from the fulfilment of everything in eternity. In any case the words, "Thy kingdom come," do not refer to an earthly paradise to be attained by scientific and technological progress in the external organization of human life. The Preface of the Mass on the feast of Christ the King explains what "Thy kingdom" is: "regnum veritatis et vitae; regnum sanctitatis et gratiae; regnum justitiae, amoris et pacis" (a kingdom of truth and of life, a kingdom of holiness and of grace, a kingdom of justice, love, and peace). This kingdom of God is clearly opposed to any this-worldliness. The fact that these words come right at the beginning of the "Our Father" is fully indicative of the absolute primacy of the supernatural, of the glorification of God.

In the words "Thy will be done on earth as it is in heaven," we enter in the deepest way into the rhythm of that which objectively ought to be. Here the main thing is to understand the meaning of "will of God."

The first meaning is: that which is pleasing to God, that which He commands us. This is the will of God which we ought to obey. The second meaning is: that which He allows. In this second sense everything which happens is God's will: happy and beautiful events as well as unhappy ones and trials and crosses and even the reign of evil.

Here we have to make an important distinction. As long as we are speaking of personal crosses such as the death of a beloved person or an incurable disease, it is a question of something allowed by God, and our response must be one of submission in which we say, "Thy will be done." We should pray to be spared personal evils as long as they can still be avoided, and we should do everything in our power to avoid them. Even our Lord prayed in Gethsemane, "If it is possible, let this cup pass from me." But then He said, "Thy will be done." If it is a question of crosses which cannot be avoided, such as the death of a beloved person, there remains for us only to say, "Thy will be done." But we have a very different case when God allows the triumph of evil in history, when He allows heresy and apostasy, and the flourishing of movements hostile to Himself such as Nazism and Communism. These are things which God allows for reasons which we cannot understand; here the words of St. Paul apply, "How incomprehensible are His judgments, how unsearchable His ways (Rom. 11:33)!"

We must not fail to grasp the call of God to fight against these evils with all our might. It would be totally false to think that God expects of us only a resigned "Thy will be done." That would be a disastrous quietism. The criterion for determining the response which God expects of us is the will of God in the first sense, in the sense of that which is pleasing to God. It would be a great, indeed a catastrophic error to think that something is pleasing to God simply because it has happened, because it has come into existence. Although we have already spoken about this dangerous error, we refer to it explicitly again.[77] It is always the will of God for us to struggle against what is evil and false. Whether we will prevail in our struggle, that we do not know, and here again we should say, "Thy will be done." As Pascal says so beautifully, we must fight with Christ, but we do not know whether we will conquer with Him. But that Christ will conquer in the end — that we know.

The response of "Thy will be done" to the crosses which God imposes on us is also according to the will of God in the first sense, in the sense of that which we should fulfill, and thereby glorify God. Thus the will of God in the first sense reaches into the sphere of the will of God in the second sense (in the sense of what God allows), at least as far as our response is concerned. But even this does not eliminate the difference between the will of God in the sense of His commandments, and the will of God in the sense of that which He allows.

But things which are not personal crosses or evils for me or others, but which are wrong and offensive to God, such as sin or apostasy or heresy, are only allowed by God for mysterious reasons, and it would be thoroughly wrong to respond by saying, "Thy will be done."

The will of God in the sense of what He allows is fulfilled in any case. In this sense of "will of God," nothing can happen against His will. And this is the sense in which a person suffering from some trial should say, "Thy will be done." We should *accept* the will of God in this sense, whereas we should *obey* the will of God in the sense of that which is pleasing to God. If we mean "will of God" in the sense of what is allowed, then it is an expression of complete abandonment to Him to say, "Thy will be done on earth as it is in heaven." The will of God in this sense is not something which ought to be, but rather only something which in any case fully exists. In thus abandoning ourselves to God we do not enter into the rhythm of that which objectively ought to be, we rather perform an act of adoring self-donation to God. But if we mean "will of God" in the sense of that which is pleasing to God, that which glorifies Him, then to say "Thy will be done" is an expression of "hungering and thirsting for justice," of "seeking first the kingdom of God," of entering into the rhythm of that which objectively ought to be. In this sense the will of God is fulfilled in heaven, there it is full reality; and thus in praying that His will be done, we enter into the rhythm of what objectively ought to be. But when we pray that the will of God be fulfilled on "earth" we are referring to something which is not yet as it ought to be. In saying "on earth *as* it is in heaven," the "as" shows clearly that heaven and the fulfillment of God's will there is taken as a model for what should be "on earth." Thus it is that in our prayer for the will of God on earth, we enter into the rhythm of that which objectively ought to be, and this is quite similar to praying, "Thy kingdom come."

But the important thing for us in the present context is that the whole first part of the Lord's Prayer is the total antithesis to this-worldliness in religion, to shifting the emphasis from eternity to earthly "progress," from the supernatural to the natural, from the glorification of God to the establishment of an earthly paradise. This whole first part concentrates on the glorification of God, and in praying it we enter deeply into the rhythm of that which objectively ought to be.

It is not until the second part of the prayer that we find the petition referring to our earthly happiness, "give us this day our daily bread." This "daily bread" refers not only to the nourishment which we need to live, but surely also to everything which is a legitimate objective good for us or for those with whom we are united in some form of love. In making this petition we clearly avoid falling into any false supernaturalism, and we see clearly that it belongs to the very nature of man to possess *Eigenleben,* that is to be interested in objective goods for himself, to yearn for happiness (I have discussed all this in Chapter IX of my book *Das Wesen der Liebe* — "The Nature of Love"). Of course, in stating clearly in the first part the absolute primacy of God and the glorification of Him, the prayer also states the absolute priority of the glorification of God over even the highest objective good for the person — that eternal beatitude which God explicitly desires for man. But as long as we are on earth we would not be full men if we were concerned *only* with the glorification of God and our eternal salvation, if we were not also interested in objective goods for ourselves such as friendship, love, marriage, the experience of what is beautiful and noble, of those goods which, since they possess high values, are precious gifts of God. We should include all these things in "our daily bread." After all even the Church prays in the litany of All Saints, *"a peste, fame et bello libera nos Domine"* (deliver us, O Lord, from plague, hunger, and war). And in the Gospel, by saying, "Ask and you will receive" (Luke 11:9), Christ is telling us to make the prayer of petition. And it is a lofty expression of our faith in the omnipotence and the infinite goodness of God to ask even for earthly goods.

We mentioned earlier that this-worldliness has nothing to do with duly appreciating all true earthly goods, it is rather a shift of emphasis from supernatural goods to natural ones. In many of my writings I have discussed the importance of earthly goods (which, since they have a high value, are sharply distinguished from merely worldly goods), and their mission to bring us closer to God; though I have never denied the danger which they have for our fallen nature, the danger of drawing us into an inordinate attachment to them. But we can understand this mission of earthly goods only in avoiding any this-worldliness, and only in recognizing the absolute primacy of the *unum necessarium* (the one thing needful).

The next petition, "forgive us our trespasses as we forgive those who trespass against us," does not also refer to earthly goods, but to our relation to God. It is an appeal to the mercy of God for the most important thing for our eternal blessedness: the forgiveness of our sins. The Psalmist speaks of the way we are thrown on the mercy of God when he says: "If you, O Lord, mark our iniquities, Lord, who can stand in your presence" (Psalm 129). It is the same appeal to the mercy of God which we find in the *Kyrie eleison,* and in the *Confiteor* when we ask our Lady and all the angels and saints to intercede for us. In this petition we return to the "one thing needful." Of course, the forgiveness of sins is not the heart of the "one thing needful"; for, this is the glorification of God. But the forgiveness of sins does refer to that great reality which comes after the glorification of God — the salvation of man, his eternal beatitude. Even if the salvation of man is second with respect to the glorification of God, still it belongs to the supernatural. We are clearly oriented to the "one thing necessary" in praying for the forgiveness of our sins, in appealing to God's mercy. In this appeal we are not concerned, as in the prayer for "our daily bread," with genuine earthly goods, but rather with our eternal salvation, with our reconciliation with God — to pray for this is precisely an expression of love for God, and of repentance for our sins.

In this part of the Lord's Prayer we also promise to forgive all those who do us wrong. Of course we all hope that God's mercy is infinitely greater than the mercy which we show to others. Our mercy is no model for God's mercy. But when we pray for the forgiveness of our sins, we have also to make the resolution to forgive "those who trespass against us," to be ready to do this, and to realize how often Christ emphasizes in the Gospel that God will forgive us and do good to us according as we forgave others and were generous with them. In this way he attaches the greatest importance to our being merciful. But in the "Our Father" we cannot ask for the forgiveness of our sins only on the condition that we "forgive those who trespass against us." These words, which express a central element of our sanctification, have more the character of a promise, of a will to forgive; they do not express a model of that mercy which we hope to receive from God and for which we pray. These words are part of a basic petition, and they express a direction of our will, a realization that forgiveness of "those who trespass against us" is a centrally important condition for our eternal beatitude. Here, too, it is eternal beatitude and our sanctification which are thematic, as well as the sweet consolation of mercy. "Blessed are the merciful, for they shall obtain mercy."

In the petition, "and lead us not into temptation," there is fully expressed the centrally important awareness of our weakness, as well as of the fact that our first task is not to offend God. Again we see clearly the full antithesis to any this-worldliness. In humbly praying that temptations to sin be kept far from us, we not only express our concern lest in our weakness we offend God, and our awareness that the most important thing for us is not to offend Him; we also express the humility which realizes that, with our own strength, we cannot avoid offending Him. Of course, the trials which God imposes on us out of love are bound up with temptations — nevertheless Christ has told us to pray to avoid temptation. We not only may but ought to make this prayer to God. It is a unique expression of humility, which is a central element of sanctity and an indispensable condition for eternal beatitude.

In the final petition, "but deliver us from evil," the theme is the sheer evil of separation from God, of eternal damnation. It is against this evil that the priest prays when he says between the *Agnus Dei* and the Communion, "And never let me be parted from Thee." Notice that it does not say, *a malis* (from evils) but *a malo* (from evil). In the Tridentine liturgy one prays after the "Our Father": "Deliver us, O Lord, from all evils, past, present, and to come." It clearly makes no sense to be freed from past evils if by evil one means earthly evils, such as crosses, pains, sufferings. How can we be freed from these when they are past? Only if evil (*malum*) refers to moral evil, to sin, to being separated from God in a way which could last for eternity, does it make sense to pray to be delivered from past evils.

But the "Our Father" speaks in the singular, it speaks of *malum* (evil), which encompasses all moral evil, all sin, all offense against God — this is that absolute evil which leads to damnation. In praying, "deliver us from evil, from wickedness" — we are praying to be delivered from the kingdom of evil. And here the whole emphasis is placed on not offending God, and on attaining to eternal beatitude. For the absolute good for us is eternal beatitude, and the absolute evil is eternal separation from God in hell.

And so we see clearly how the prayer which Christ taught the Apostles and, through them, all Christians, is the clearest proof that this-worldliness is unmistakably the antithesis to the Christian Revelation, and in fact apostasy from Christ.

NOTES

77. Thus Kierkegaard: "So one errs also in supposing that what happens, for the mere fact that it happens, indicates God's approving consent." Quoted by Lowrie, *Kierkegaard* (New York: Harper, 1962), vol. II, p. 551.

27

How God Wants Us to Respond in the Present Crisis

AND NOW ARISES AGAIN the great question of conscience for us: how should we respond in the present situation when the vineyard of the Lord is devastated? We already posed this question in discussing the distortion of the sacred humanity of Christ, which is perhaps the worst part of the devastation of the vineyard. And now we return to this question, which is so important, and we ask what the right attitude is for each individual who clearly recognizes the full, terrible extent of this devastation.

It would be thoroughly false to say: since God allows it, it must be according to His will, and so we have nothing to do but say, "Thy will be done," even if this devastation breaks our heart. At the basis of this attitude is that equivocation with the term "the will of God" which we uncovered in meditating on the "Our Father." When God allows something of a great disvalue, such as the triumph of evil, or apostasy, or heresy, it would not be the right response to say, "Thy will be done." As St. Paul says, God allows these evils in order to test us. But it is a deadly and radically false notion to think that, because God allows heresies to be readily spread, we should not fight against them but should go along with them in a spirit of resignation. This is a false interpretation of resignation to God's will. The devastation of the vineyard of the Lord should instead fill us with the deepest pain, and mobilize us for the fight, to be fought with all legitimate means, against everything which is evil and offensive to God, against all heresies.

A second false response would be that of resignation, "It is a terrible source of grief that the Church is in such a state of disintegration, but how can we possibly put a stop to this process?" In this attitude of despair one gives up all hope of a "second spring" in the vineyard of the Lord. One throws up one's hands in despair, and is even in danger of separating in spirit from the Church. Such people are in danger of being so scandalized by the unfortunate new missal and especially by the elimination of the Tridentine Mass that they think that they no longer have the duty of attending Sunday Mass if it is in the *Novus Ordo*. But just the contrary is true: necessary as it is to recognize and to suffer under the spirit and the tendency which is at the basis of these changes in the liturgy — and we cannot help saying that these changes have disfigured the holy Mass — nevertheless the right response from us is to strengthen our faith in the real bodily presence of our Lord in the Sacrament, and to desire more deeply than ever to attend Mass and receive Communion every day. And by the way, we should not let ourselves be diverted by new formulations and by the elimination of important prayers, from what is objectively present at

Mass. For instance, we must not forget the Tridentine *Confiteor* in which we accuse ourselves before God and before the whole court of heaven, since objectively our sins offend God and not the parish community, and objectively the important thing is to enter into the invisible world of heaven.[78]

Padre Pio told a friend of mine who was deploring many of the liturgical changes, "You are right — but Christ has not abandoned us. He is still present in the tabernacle, and the Holy Sacrifice still takes place objectively!" And so it is clear that the attitude of resignation, of despair over the Church, is not the right response.

A third false response, and perhaps the most dangerous one, would be to imagine that there is no devastation of the vineyard of the Lord, that it only seems so to us — our task as laymen is simply to adhere with complete loyalty to whatever our bishop says and not to dare to pass judgment on all those things which I have referred to in this book as elements of the devastation of the vineyard of the Lord. This is the attitude which, as mentioned above, is demanded precisely by the bishops who pursue an ostrich-policy of willful blindness and who as a result regard as annoying disturbers of the peace all those who protest against heresies and the devastation of the Church.

At the basis of this attitude is a false idea of loyalty to the hierarchy. When the pope speaks *ex cathedra* on faith or morals, then unconditional acceptance and submission is required of every Catholic. But it is false to extend this loyalty to encyclicals in which *new* theses are proposed. This is not to deny that the magisterium of the Church extends much farther than the dogmas. If an encyclical deals with a question of faith or morals and is based on the tradition of the holy Church — that is, expresses something which the Church has always taught — then we should humbly accept its teaching. This is the case with the encyclical *Humanae Vitae*: although we do not have here the strict infallibility of a defined dogma, the content of the encyclical nevertheless belongs to that sphere of the Church's magisterium which we must accept as true.

But there are many encyclicals which deal with very different (e.g., sociological) questions and which express a response of the Church to certain new conditions. Thus the encyclical of the great Pope Pius XI, *Quadragesimo Anno,* with its idea of a corporate state, differs on sociological questions with encyclicals of Paul VI. But when it is a question of practical ordinances such as concordats, or the suppression of the Jesuit order by Pope Clement XIV, or the introduction of the new missal, or the rearrangement of the Church calendar, or the new rubrics for the liturgy, then our obedience (as Vatican I declares[79]), but by no means our agreement is required (I made this distinction in my article in *Triumph,* March, 1970). In the history of the Church there have been many unfortunate ordinances and practical decisions by popes, which have then been retracted by other popes. In such matters we may, while obeying an ordinance, with all due respect express opposition to it, pray for its elimination, and address many appeals to the pope.

This holds even more for the ordinances of a bishop, especially in a time when there are bishops who belong to a kind of "fifth column" in the Church, and when there are many other bishops who, while not belonging to it, nevertheless fear public opinion more than God, and thus always swim with the tide of the times, or at least do not dare to take up the fight against the prevailing tendencies.

No, none of these responses is the one which God expects

of us. Our response must be rather a growth in faith, hope, and charity. Is not the devastation of the vineyard of the Lord an exhortation to love God, Christ, and His holy Church more than ever? Do we not betray Christ if we turn away in disgust? Should not *we* of all people strive to see that true beauty of the vineyard of the Lord, which objectively continues to exist despite the devastation? So our response must be to work for the glorification of God, and toward our own personal sanctification, and to oppose this-worldliness by our own unconditional imitation of Christ.

This has, of course, become more difficult. We are no longer surrounded by the radiance of the holy Church as we were before the Council. When we attended a solemn high Mass, what an indescribable atmosphere of holy truth we breathed, how we supported in our faith, how we were drawn into the world of Christ. Today our faith no longer has this support and help, it has to penetrate through much which is foreign to this sacred world in order to reach that tremendous and sacred event, the mystery of the unbloody re-enactment of Calvary, and of the union of love between our soul and Jesus in Communion. This is precisely why the devastation of the vineyard of the Lord is a time when our faith is tried, when we are called upon to grow in faith, hope, and love. But it is a time of trial which demands a completely new kind of watchfulness, and this leads to a further response which we must give.

We have to realize that our time is like the time of Arianism, and so we have to be extremely careful lest we be poisoned ourselves without noticing it. We must not underestimate the power of those ideas which fill the intellectual atmosphere of the time, nor the danger of being infected by them when we are daily breathing this atmosphere. Nor should we underestimate the danger of getting used to the evils of the times, and then becoming insensitive to them. At first perhaps many people see the devastation of the vineyard, and react in the right way. But *gutta cavat lapidem* (dripping water slowly erodes the stone) — after a while one becomes accustomed to it. Then, too, there is this to consider, that the devastation of the vineyard is an increasing process, and so certain evils which belong to the earlier stages, seem harmless in the light of the later stages. And so we are in danger of becoming insensitive, on the one hand, because we get used to the devastation, and on the other hand, because the devastation progresses, and its beginnings seem insignificant in the light of its advanced forms.

But it is still worse to become infected than to be insensitive. The first thing to be done in order to avoid both dangers is to realize completely how extraordinary is the situation in which we live today. St. Peter tells us, "Brethren, be watchful, be sober, for your adversary the devil goes about like a roaring lion, seeking someone to devour" (1 Peter 5:8). Just fifty years ago this watchfulness mainly referred to our temptations to sin, to the danger of offending God by sins of impurity, pharisaism, pride, greed, ambition, lack of charity, disobedience to the commands of God. Of course, even then there was the danger of being tempted by those intellectual and spiritual trends of the time which were incompatible with the revelation of Christ — but those dangers were outside the Church, and the danger for a Catholic was to fall away from the Church under their influence (and this happened often enough).

But today these trends are able to develop within the Church. We can clearly discern them in sermons, in pastoral letters, and in books by well-known theologians. Since these bad trends encounter so little resistance within the Church, it has become much more difficult for the simple faithful to grasp their incompatibility with the deposit of faith.[80] Thus St. Peter's exhortation to watchfulness applies today in a special way to watchfulness with respect to heresies within the Church. We must constantly determine whether sermons, or new books of Catholic theologians, do not contain something heretical, or some basically false emphasis. The *Imprimatur* used to be a great guarantee, and especially the Index. But today we have to develop in ourselves a special awareness, a holy mistrust, for we not only live in a poisoned world, but in a devastated Church. In our present trial God requires of us this watchfulness, this holy fear of being infected. It would be a lack of humility to think that we are in no danger of being infected. It would be a false security rooted in pride if we were to think that we are immune. Each of us must become aware of his frailty, and understand that this special watchfulness is required of us by God in the trial which we are going through.

It is important to realize that this is not the first time when Catholics have had to go through this trial. Cardinal Newman tells us:

"It is a miserable time when a man's Catholic profession is no voucher for his orthodoxy, and when a teacher of religion may be within the Church's pale, yet external to her faith. Such has been for a season the trial of her children at various eras of her history. It was the state of things during the dreadful Arian ascendancy, when the flock had to keep aloof from the shepherd, and the unsuspicious Fathers of the Western Councils trusted and followed some consecrated sophist from Greece or Syria. It was the case in those passages of medieval history when simony resisted the Supreme

Pontiff, or when heresy lurked in the universities. It was a longer and more tedious trial, while the controversies lasted with the Monophysites of old, and with the Jansenists in modern times. A great scandal it is and a perplexity to the little ones of Christ, to have to choose between rival claimants upon their allegiance, or to find a condemnation at length pronounced upon one whom in their simplicity they have admired." [81]

In the present time, "when a teacher of religion may be within the Church's pale, yet external to her faith," we must nourish ourselves with the thought of the great theologians of the past, with the works of St. Augustine, St. Anselm, St. Thomas, St. Francis de Sales, Cardinal Newman. Let us arm our souls against the theological poison of the times, by reading those condemnations of errors which were pronounced by Trent and Vatican I. Let us read the Credo of our Holy Father Pope Paul VI. Let us sharpen our sense of the specifically supernatural ethos by reading the lives of the saints. Let us preserve a lively contact with the saints, let us ask them to intercede for us.

And then we have to fight with all our strength — each of us according to his own possibilities — against all the heresies which are being spread every day without being explicitly condemned, without being anathematized, and without the heretics themselves being excommunicated. Phrases about "the unity of Catholics" must not hinder us from taking up this holy struggle. Let us not forget that St. Francis de Sales, the saint of meekness, admonishes us in his *Introduction to the Devout Life*, "Here I am especially speaking of the open enemies of God and His Church; they must be publically branded just as often as possible. It is a deed of love to cry the alarm when the wolf breaks into the sheepfold" (Part III, Chap. 29).

Of course an important part of this struggle is the "apostolate of being," that is, the great responsibility that every Christian has before God of giving witness for Christ not only by what he says and does, but also by what he is. In this sense every Christian is called to the apostolate, and is partially responsible for the soul of his neighbor.

And contemplation must play a role in the life of every Christian if he is to be a real apostle, although the role of contemplation varies for each Christian, according to his particular calling.

When we realize all this, when we consider the lives of the saints and the unadulterated teaching of the holy Church, we cannot help seeing what real renewal consists in, and how we can awaken and give new life to our faith, to our lives as Christians.

So we see that God expects us, in the present devastation of His vineyard, to respond first of all by growing in faith, hope, and love; secondly, by being especially watchful lest we be infected in any way; thirdly, by struggling against the devastation with all the means at our disposal; and fourthly, by not forgetting that the absolute truth of the deposit of the Catholic Faith objectively remains untouched by all the empty talk of certain theologians. The "world" radiated by the Tridentine Mass and by Gregorian Chant objectively remains the true, blissful world which awaits us in eternity. The incomprehensible holiness and beauty of the sacred humanity of Jesus remains a great objective reality despite all the attempts at secularization and desacralization.

We must never forget that in spite of all diabolic devastation of the vineyard of the Lord, the glory of the holy Church, the bride of Christ, and the glory of all the saints nevertheless remains untouched in its reality, indeed it is the one true reality. What do all the changing trends of the time really amount to? They are so much "sound and fury, signifying nothing" when compared with the eternal truth and the objective glory of Jesus Christ, with the holiness of the saints which glorifies God. Of course, it is terrible to see the vineyard of the Lord ravaged, to see the souls of innocent children poisoned by outrageous catechisms and by "sex education"; we cannot shed enough tears over all this, we cannot fight fiercely enough against it with all the resources at our disposal. And yet, holy joy must awaken in us because we know what the truth of the Redemption is, because God is and remains the same God who is revealed to us by Christ and His holy Church in the deposit of the Catholic Faith. The true sacred humanity of Christ, of which we find a reflection in all the saints, remains the same.

> Jesu nostra redemptio
> Amor et desiderium
> Deus Creator omnium
> Homo in fine temporum.
>
> Tu esto nostrum gaudium,
> Qui es futurus praemium:
> Sit nostra in te gloria
> Per cuncta semper saecula. Amen.[82]

NOTES

78. When I say that it was an unfortunate change to eliminate all mention of the saints in the first part of the new *Confiteor*, and to replace them with the parish community, one should not object that the priest in the Tridentine *Confiteor* turned to the congregation and said, *et vobis fratres* (and to you, my brothers). For in the dialogue between priest and congregation it was quite meaningful for the priest to accuse himself be-

fore those people who are entrusted to his spiritual care. And in monasteries and convents there is a deep meaning in confessing to the others in the *Confiteor,* since the religious of a monastery form a kind of family whose members live together.

One should also not object that our sins are after all a wrong committed against the whole Church, the mystical Body. For this is not at all adequately expressed in the vernacular phrase, "and you, my brothers and sisters."

79. The duty of this obedience is made clear by the dogmatic constitution *Pastor Aeternus* of Vatican I: "And so we teach and declare that in the disposition of God the Roman Pontiff holds the pre-eminence of ordinary power over all other churches, and that this power of jurisdiction of the Roman Pontiff, which is truly episcopal, is immediate. Regarding this jurisdiction the shepherds of whatever rite and dignity, and the faithful individually and collectively, are bound by the duty of hierarchical submission and sincere obedience. And this holds not only for matters relating to faith and morals, but also to matters pertaining to the discipline and government of the Church throughout the whole world." (Ch. 3; Denz. 1827).

80. I was quite astonished when a deeply devout Catholic friend told me how enthusiastic she was about a study group to which she belonged which was reading the works of Teilhard de Chardin. Though an intelligent and educated person, she nevertheless found Teilhard to be wonderful, and did not notice how absolutely incompatible his theories are with the teaching of the holy Church. But I was able to change her mind on this.

81. John Henry Cardinal Newman, *The Idea of a University,* "A Form of Infidelity of the Day," par. 2, section 1.

82. From the Hymn of Vespers on the Feast of the Ascension. One English translation renders these lines as follows:

> Hail, thou who man's Redeemer art,
> Jesu, the joy of every heart;
> Great Maker of the world's wide frame,
> And purest love's delight and flame.
> Our guide, our way to heavenly rest,
> Be thou the aim of every breast;
> Be thou the soother of our tears,
> Our sweet reward in endless years.   Amen.